THE

JURISDICTION AND MISSION

OF THE

Anglican Episcopate.

BY THE

REV. T. J. BAILEY, B.A.,

C. C. COLL., CAMBRIDGE,

AUTHOR OF "A DEFENCE OF HOLY ORDERS,"

ETC., ETC.

LONDON: J. & J. H. PARKER, 337, STRAND;

NEW YORK: POTT & AMERY, COOPER UNION.

1871.

TO

HIS GRACE

THE RIGHT HONOURABLE AND MOST REVEREND

ARCHIBALD CAMPBELL TAIT,

D.D., D.C.L., LL.D,

LORD ARCHBISHOP OF CANTERBURY, PRIMATE OF ALL ENGLAND,

AND METROPOLITAN,

ETC., ETC., ETC.,

THIS TREATISE,

WITH EARNEST THANKS FOR HIS GREAT KINDNESS

TO THE AUTHOR

DURING THE PREPARATION OF HIS WORK ON

"THE DEFENCE OF HOLY ORDERS,"

IS

MOST RESPECTFULLY DEDICATED

BY

THE AUTHOR.

PREFACE.

Any contribution, however small, to the efforts now being made by those to whom the Church and her welfare is the dearest object in life, to place that Church in her true aspect before the world, will, it is hoped, be accepted in the spirit in which it is offered.

It is in this spirit that this brief treatise upon that confessedly difficult and misunderstood subject, "the Jurisdiction and Mission" of the Anglican Episcopate, is put forth by the Author. It is also in fulfilment of a hope expressed by him in his "Defence of Holy Orders in the Church of England," to be able at some future time to enter more fully upon the question than he did there in the fourth chapter of that work. At the same time it is by no means intended as an exhaustive treatise; indeed, such a mass of materials from which to draw matter and illustration were at hand, that a work of almost any size might have been compiled; but his object was rather to present in a popular and readable form an analysis of the various opinions of Canonists and great Divines of the Church in various ages upon this subject.

T. J. BAILEY.

Runnymede House,
Brighton,
March 31, 1871.

CONTENTS.

JURISDICTION AND MISSION.

SECTION I.

THE question of the Jurisdiction and Mission of the Bishops of the Anglican Church is not only one of the utmost importance of itself, but derives a further importance from the fact that one of the objections most pertinaciously and determinedly urged against the Church of England since the Reformation, is, that she has no true jurisdiction or mission. The object of the following treatise is an endeavour to show, by reference to eminent authorities, and an enquiry into the historical facts at the period of Archbishop Parker's elevation to the Primatial See of Canterbury, that every condition required by the Canon Law of the Church has been scrupulously fulfilled with the utmost care, and that in consequence the prelates of the Anglican Church are possessed of jurisdiction and mission (and that too entirely independent of the State) as real as was ever possessed by any Bishop since the time of the Apostles.

This statement, which many persons may be tempted to regard as somewhat bold and presumptuous, I make without any reservation whatever, 1st, Because I am convinced that an impartial study of the Canon Law of the Church, the decrees of her various councils, and the writings of such great canonists as Van Espen, De Marca, Thomassinus, and others, can lead to no other conclusion than this; and 2ndly, Because a great cause of the apparent confidence of those who allege our want of jurisdiction, arises from the manner in which the subject itself has often been treated

B

by writers upon it. Not only has the ordinary meaning of the word been misunderstood, but a well-nigh inextricable confusion seems to have possession of the minds of some of them, jurisdiction and mission being spoken of as one and interchangeable—no distinction being made between habitual and actual jurisdiction—and some again speaking of jurisdiction as being conferred at one time, some at another; and here let me add that I leave out of the question, as simply untenable, the Ultramontane theory of jurisdiction flowing simply from the Pope.

Bearing, then, these two reasons in mind, I desire to lay down the broad principle upon which every argument which I venture to adduce must be built, "that every Bishop has universal mission and universal jurisdiction by virtue of his integral share in the apostolic office and commission conveyed to him by consecration." This being premised, the question of local mission and local jurisdiction, whether Diocesan, Metropolitical, or Patriarchal, becomes, comparatively, an easy matter.

That the Apostles, by virtue of their commission from Christ Himself, received universal mission and jurisdiction is beyond dispute from the words of Holy Scripture itself. "All power (Ἐξουσία, 'power, authority, jurisdiction, rule') is given unto me in heaven and in earth. Go ye therefore, and teach (disciple) all nations, baptising them . . . . . teaching them to observe all things whatsoever I have commanded you: and lo, I am with you alway, even unto the end of the world." [*S. Matt.* xxviii. 18,19.] Again—"As my Father hath sent me, even so send I you. And when He had said this, He breathed on them and said unto them, Receive ye the Holy Ghost. Whosesoever sins ye remit they are remitted unto them, and whosesoever sins ye retain they are retained."

"From these passages it is certain, in the first place," says the learned Father Antonio Pereira, "that by virtue of this mission, which Christ gave to His Apostles, they were constituted ministers of the New Testament, as S. Paul calls them [2 *Cor.* iii. 6], *i.e.*, the shepherds of His Church, and administrators or dispensers of all the sacraments which the Lord Himself instituted, and of which He makes mention only of baptism and penance. . . . . It is certain, in the second place, that this administration of the sacraments includes not only the power of order, but also that of jurisdiction; that is, not only the power of consecrating the body of Christ, and of absolving from sin, but also the administration of these and of the other sacraments, the choice and mission of fresh ministers, the power of establishing new laws concerning such administration of the sacraments, and consequently the power of dispensation in respect of such laws at all times when the advantage or necessities of the faithful required it. Therefore S. Paul explains the office of a Bishop to consist in ruling and governing the Church of God. 'Take heed to yourselves, and to the flock, over which the Holy Ghost hath made you Bishops to rule the Church of God,' [*Acts* xx. 28]; and it is evident that from this governing power, the power of establishing laws, and consequently that of dispensing with them, cannot be separated." [*Tent. Theol., pp.* 31, 32; *Transl. by Landon. Edit.* 1847.]

This power of universal mission and jurisdiction was exercised by the Apostles until their deaths, and the position of the Church is thus set forth by Van Espen:

"These first Apostles were by Christ Himself, as I have said, elected and appointed to this office; who also, that they might, in some manner, be perpetual in the Church, gave to them the power of choosing and appointing others to the same work as He had chosen and appointed them. He said therefore to them, 'As My Father hath sent me, so send I you' [*S. John* xx. 21], with a general commission and command, that as He had from the Father a general command to teach, instruct and convert the world to the knowledge of the true God, and of deputing the ministers necessary for this, furnished with the necessary authority, so they also might have the same office and command, with the same authority for choosing ministers furnished with like authority; and that with a continual succession to the end of the world.

"The Apostles, therefore, by the authority delegated to them by Christ, transferred to the Bishops as their lawful successors whatever was necessary for the due administration of the Church.

"Hence, S. Augustine (on Psalm xliv.) expounds thus that

passage of the Psalmist, 'Instead of thy fathers, children have been born to thee:'—'The Apostles were sent to thee as fathers: instead of the Apostles, sons have been born to thee; there have been appointed Bishops. For in the present day, whence do the Bishops throughout all the world derive their origin? The Church itself calls them fathers; the Church itself brought them forth, and placed them on the thrones of the fathers. Think not thyself abandoned, then, because thou seest not Peter, nor seest Paul; seest not those through whom thou wert born. Out of thine own offspring has a body of 'fathers' been raised up to thee; instead of thy fathers, have children been born to thee.' And S. Cyprian [*Ep* 24, *Oxford Ed. Ep.* 45]: 'For this, my brother, we especially both labour after, and ought to labour after, to be careful to maintain, as much as we can, the unity delivered by the Lord, and through His Apostles to us their successors.' The Bishops, therefore, succeed to the authority of the Apostles so certainly, that whatever Episcopal power (that is, pertaining to the government of the Church) the Apostles had, this was transferred by them to the Bishops, as their successors in the administration and government of the Church.

"But those things which belong to the Apostles, not as Bishops, but as Apostles, neither are necessary to the due government and administration of the Church (unless, perhaps, for the time being), do not pass on to the Bishops; neither in these do they succeed the Apostles: so that on that account they are called not Apostles, but simply Bishops. In fine, they succeed the Apostles in the ministerial power of ecclesiastical government, but by no means in this, that they are witnesses, and truly eye-witnesses, of the life, doctrine, and resurrection of Jesus Christ our Lord; nor in this, that they are chosen immediately by Christ, and sent to preach the Gospel; neither in many graces and prerogatives, as in the abundance of the Holy Spirit, in infallibility of doctrine, in plenitude of wisdom, in the gift of tongues and of miracles, etc. For in these things, which were the special properties of the Apostles, no ordinary succession is given in the Church; for these were gifts and privileges of the Apostolate properly so called, to which the Bishops did not succeed: but whatever else of power and office the Apostles had, that was entirely the property of the Episcopate, and plenarily transferred to the Bishops, as their successors, for the government of their future dioceses.

"The Episcopate contains *per se* full power of Ecclesiastical government and the plenitude of the Priesthood; but after the death of the Apostles, as S. Cyprian says, a portion of the flock was assigned to each pastor, which he should rule and govern. This discipline seemed so necessary for avoiding confusion, that the Church has preserved it even to the present day, and frequently confirmed it by various canons; and has strongly forbidden the Bishops to order or do anything in another diocese, without the permission of the Bishop of that diocese." [*Van Espen; Jur. Ecclesi., Pars.* 1, *Tit.* 16, *c.* 1, §§ 4, 5, 6, 7, 8, 9.]

"Accordingly," says a writer in the *Union Review* for 1866, "the perpetual universal mission and jurisdiction of the Apostolic College inheres in the Episcopate; for 'the spirit of Elijah doth rest on Elisha,' and the one is the legitimate descendant, successor, and representative of the other." It is, however, to S. Cyprian, the great Doctor of the Church, that we instinctively turn; and the principle which he continually maintains and insists on in all his actions and writings is thus briefly summed up by the writer quoted above:—"That the Church is one, and the Episcopate one; that all Bishops are by divine appointment equal, both in power and authority, as joint rulers of one spiritual kingdom; all having an equal and that a perfect share in the one and undivided Episcopate. That every one is therefore equal to all others individually, but inferior to them collectively; and wherever the collective authority does not interpose, each one is independent in the discharge of his episcopal functions." [*Union Review*, 1866.] The passages themselves from S. Cyprian are too well known to require insertion in full; suffice it to quote one or two passages. "And though He gives to all the Apostles an equal power, and says, 'As my Father sent Me, even so send I you,' etc., [*S. John* xx. 21—23]; yet, in order to manifest unity, He has by His own authority so placed the source of the same unity as to begin from one. Certainly the other Apostles also were what Peter was, endued with an equal fellowship both of honour and power; but a commencement is made from unity, that the Church may be set before us as one." [*De Unit. Eccl. Oxford Trans., p.* 134; *Edit.* 1846.] And again in the same treatise he adds: "The Episcopate is one: it is a whole, in which each enjoys full possession."

In the 27th Epistle, "Ad Lapsos," he says it has been established by Divine law, "that the Church should be built upon the Bishops, and that every act of the Church should be governed by the same rulers;" while in his 72nd Epistle to Pope S. Stephen, he writes that each Bishop is supreme prelate in his own diocese; "every head possesses the free exercise of his will in the administration of his Church, subject to the account which he must hereafter render of his deeds unto the Lord."

To these quotations from S. Cyprian, which seem to bear out the truth of what has been stated, I cannot forbear adding the very valuable note to the treatise "On the Unity of the Church," in the Oxford translation of S. Cyprian's treatises, p. 150:—"Our Divines then consider that the Church is one, and that, as there is but one Bishop Invisible, so in theory there is but one visible Bishop, the type of the Invisible, how many soever there actually are; each separate individual Bishop being but a reiteration of every other, and as if but one out of innumerable shadows cast by one and the same object; each being sovereign and supreme over the whole flock of Christ, as if there were none other but himself. Such is the theory of the Apostolical system; but in order to avoid the differences of opinion and action, and consequent schism, which the actual multiplicity of governors would occasion, certain ecclesiastical regulations have from the first been observed, accommodating the abstract theory to the actual state of human nature, as we find it. First, Bishops have been restrained, as regards Christ's flock, into local districts called Dioceses; next, as regards each other, by the institution of synodal meetings or councils, the united decisions of which bind each Bishop as if it was his own individual decision; and moreover, still for the sake of order, by prescribed rules of precedence. . . . Accordingly, when S. Peter is said to be the *head* of the Church, whether in Scripture or the Fathers, we interpret it of his representing the *abstract* Bishop, the one and only ruler who is put over the household, that which each Bishop is by office, nay, and is actually, except so far as he is shackled by what may be called the bye-laws of the Divine polity."

This idea of the indivisible unity of the Episcopate is further noticed by Van Espen, when he says, "Inasmuch as all the Apostles, by virtue of their mission, which they had received from Christ, were bound to preach the Gospel throughout the whole world; so also the Bishops their successors, notwithstanding this allotment to a certain Church, are considered to be called to bestow the pastoral care upon all the faithful, and to preach the Gospel to every creature, when necessity or the welfare of our neighbour shall so require." [*Van Espen; Jur. Eccl., P.* 1, *Tit.* xvi., *c.* vi., § 1.]

These extracts from the Fathers and Canonists of the Church might be extended at pleasure; it will, however, perhaps seem sufficient to add, that the learned Thomassinus, in his great work "De Beneficiis," abounds in passages which declare that the Bishops are in the fullest sense of the word successors of the Apostles, not only as regards "order, but jurisdiction and government, which they have received from the institution of Christ Himself:" and in order to strengthen what he has himself affirmed of the power of the Bishops, he remarks that no one has spoken more soundly or profoundly of this doctrine—viz., the perfection of the Episcopate—than the great Parisian theologian, Petrus Aurelius; who says: "Christ instituted the Episcopal office, not maimed or mutilated, but a full, entire, and perfect office—the highest and most perfect image of His own highest and most perfect Priesthood. For the Bishop represents Christ and acts as His substitute on earth, as the Holy Fathers constantly affirm. As, therefore, the Priesthood of Christ contains the whole sacerdotal authority and the full power of feeding the flock, so the various powers included in that plenitude and fulness may be distinguished and discerned, but cannot be dissociated or in any way separated without grievous sin; so the Episcopate, in its very nature, contains the plenitude of the Priesthood and the fulness of the Pastoral office; and the office has been endowed with such dignity by Christ, that he who should endeavour to separate and sever the great power belonging to so high a dignity would be as guilty as if he should disjoin the properties of Christ's Priesthood and of His actual

Divine nature, and would obliterate the most excellent image of Christ on earth. For Christ received the fulness of the Priesthood from the Father when He was sent by Him; wherefore He gave the fulness of the same Priesthood, or both the powers of the Episcopate, at the same time, to the Apostles, when He sent them as the Father had sent Him. Afterwards they handed down the same fulness of authority to the Bishops; sending them as they themselves had been sent by Christ: which same fulness the Bishops lastly transmitted to those who came after them; sending these as they had been sent by the Apostles." [*Pet. Aurel., Vind. Cens. Sorbonne, T.* ii., *p.* 87.] From this quotation we gather the view of the question which presented itself to his mind; and this view is supported by his other writings, in which he shows that, although the power of order and the power of jurisdiction in Bishops may be in themselves distinct, it by no means follows that these powers can be at will separated. Certainly it must be admitted that his argument was directed against the claim made by the Popes of universal jurisdiction inherent in the See of S. Peter and flowing immediately from Christ Himself: but his argument is by no means to be limited to this alone, but bears equally upon what has been now set forth as to the universal jurisdiction and mission of each individual Bishop by virtue of this commission. And so he goes on to show that "by the institution of Christ the power of jurisdiction was so closely connected with that of order, that in the understanding and acceptation of the Primitive Church a Bishop deprived of jurisdiction was actually regarded in the light of a layman." [*Pereira, Tent. Theol., p.* 45.]

If, then, this theory of the universal jurisdiction and mission of each Bishop be a true one, nothing can weaken the strength of the proposition, that in the (well-nigh) impossible supposition of the death of all the Bishops in a kingdom save one, that one, by virtue of his Apostolic commission, would be fully competent (not merely from the extreme necessity of the case, but as a matter of strict legality in accordance with the rights which he possessed *qua Episcopus*) to consecrate other Bishops, and give them all that was needed of jurisdiction and mission.

SECTION II.

Having thus briefly laid down the broad basis upon which all jurisdiction and mission is founded, I propose now to examine the question as applied to the exercise of that jurisdiction—(actual jurisdiction, that is, as distinguished from habitual jurisdiction)—and mission as possessed by the prelates of our Church; and in doing so it will be necessary first to define the terms, and then to enquire when and how the powers which they convey are given to the possessors of them: and to this end reference will be made to, and our information drawn from, the laws and practice of the early Church. And here let me quote the valuable words of Bishop Gibson, in the Introduction to his Codex:—

"Canon law is partly foreign and partly domestic. The Foreign is what is commonly called the Body of Canon Law, consisting of the Canons of Councils, Decrees of Popes, and the like, which obtained in England, by virtue of their own authority (in like manner as they did in the other parts of the Western Church), till the time of the Reformation; and from that time have continued upon the foot of *Consent, Usage, and Custom.* For which distinction we have no less warrant than an Act of Parliament, made at the very time when these laws were declared to be no longer binding by their own authority.

"'Where this, your grace's realm, recognising no superiority under God, but only your grace, hath been and is free from subjection to any man's laws, but only to such as have been devised, made, and obtained within this realm, for the wealth of the same, or to each other as by sufferance of your grace and your progenitors, the people of this your realm have taken at their free liberty, by their own consent to be used amongst them, and have bound themselves by long use and custom to the observance of the same, not as to the observance of laws of any foreign prince, potentate, or prelate, but as to the customed and ancient laws of this realm, originally established as laws of the same, by the said sufferance, consents, and customs, and none otherwise.' [25 *Hen. VIII.*, *c.* 21, § 1.]

"Here we have a plain declaration that Foreign Laws become part of the Law of England by long use and custom.

And as the Church of England, in many cases, both of voluntary and contentious jurisdiction, had no other rule by which to proceed, so in admitting and practising the rules which they found there, they had no restraints upon them, save these two: that they were adapted to the constitution of this Church, and so were proper rules; and not contradicted by the laws of the land, and so were legal rules. Which last was the condition of their being received and practised here, as well before the Reformation as since." [*Gibson, Introd. to Codex.*]

"Jurisdiction," says Ferraris, [*Prompta Bibliotheca*] "is defined as the faculty of any one having public authority and pre-eminence over others for their guidance and government. It is derived *a jure dicendo*, according to justice and the rules of law, which is one of the principal offices of public power." It is divided into civil and ecclesiastical. As, therefore, our object is an enquiry into the latter, we shall omit any further reference to the former which is concerned with secular causes and the temporal rule of the state.

"Ecclesiastical jurisdiction is concerned with causes pertaining to the worship of God and the spiritual care of souls, and this jurisdiction is exercised (1) in the *forum externum* of the courts; and (2) in the *forum internum* of conscience and the sacraments. It is further divided into voluntary and contentious, of which voluntary is that which is exercised only over willing subjects, and to this in things civil pertain manumission and adoption; but in things sacred Ordination, Consecration, Benediction, Absolution, Dispensation, Collation of Benefices, and the like. Contentious jurisdiction is that which is exercised against unwilling subjects, viz., in appealing to law, punishing and exercising other powers of this kind, which cannot be done except in the court of a judge, whether a suit arises between two or more."

The learned Archdeacon Mason likewise thus treats of jurisdiction:—"Episcopal jurisdiction extends properly to causes spiritual or ecclesiastical only; and a Bishop, as Bishop, handleth ecclesiastical causes in an ecclesiastical manner, as having authority of himself, as in the right of his *ordinary office, not only* to minister the Word and Sacraments in the Church of God, but also to perform other holy and solemn actions; such as the Ordination of Ministers, Excommunication, and Absolution. . . . One part of jurisdiction is called internal, consisting in the administration of God's Holy Word, and Sacraments; the other external, which is both coercitive and directive: coercitive, in inflicting the censure of Excommunication, Suspension, and the like; directive, consisting in the power to make canons and constitutions, relating to the cure and direction of souls, and the right adminstration of the Sacraments." [*Mason, Vind., bk.* 4, *c.* 1, 2.]

Spozzius defines the power of Episcopal order, dignity, and jurisdiction as follows:—"Of Order,—to bless and consecrate churches, altars, chalices, oratories, cemeteries, and other places; vestments, bells, linen, and vessels used in divine worship, to reconcile the same when desecrated; to bless and consecrate Abbots and Monks; to prepare the Chrism, the oil for the sick, and the Catechumens on Holy Thursday; to confirm boys and girls already baptized, to ordain the Clergy, to exercise pontifical rights," etc. Of jurisdiction,—"To exercise authority over those subject to them, to receive oaths of canonical obedience from them, to confirm those subject to them who have been elected to benefices, to form new parishes and erect colleges, to rectify those already formed; to restore Churches fallen to decay, and to transfer some of them to the rank of Mother Churches; to elect, present, institute those presented, to deprive, to unite benefices, to confer them; to receive resignations, to take cognisance of and adjudicate on matters pertaining to the Episcopal court; to visit, to reform, to ordain, to issue edicts, constitutions and precepts; to prosecute, incarcerate, torture, condemn delinquents, punish with perpetual imprisonment, fine; excommunicate, absolve, suspend, interdict, depose, degrade; to hand over to the secular court those degraded; to invoke the secular arm; to mitigate and fix punishments, administer the oath of purgation; to pardon delinquents, to remit penalties in reserved cases, to carry out pious wishes, and other the like which pertain to Episcopal jurisdiction." [*Spozzius de Episc., bk.* 2, *qu* 2, 3, 4, *fol.* 39.]

Barbosa, Protonotary Apostolic, Bishop of Ugentino,

formerly Referee of the Sacred Congregation of the Index, thus writes :—"In Bishops there is a twofold power, one of Order, the other of Jurisdiction. The power of Order is of all Sacraments, consecrating the Chrism, exercising the office of preaching, ordaining others, preparing for the reception of the Eucharist, and creating Priests. But of them as of Priests there is one final cause, viz., the Consecration of the Most Holy Eucharist . . . whence, as may be seen in the Rubric in the Roman Pontifical concerning the Consecration of a Bishop, to the power of Episcopal order, three things properly and fully pertain, viz., to Ordain, Consecrate, and Confirm. . . . But the power of Jurisdiction has regard to the mystical body of the faithful, to whom, scattered throughout the world, it was fit that Bishops and Præfects should be assigned, in proportion to the extent of districts, and the population of kingdoms, of which Bishops some had a greater, some a less power of jurisdiction in making laws, as necessity or utility seemed to demand. This power of jurisdiction is usually divided into that which pertains to the Episcopal dignity, viz., taking cognizance of matrimonial causes, inflicting public penances, etc.; and into that which is called simpler jurisdiction; to judge, excommunicate, correct, receive oaths, confirm, invest, confer benefices, institute, and other such like. . . . Between the two classes of jurisdiction there is this difference, that of those things which pertain to the Episcopal dignity, a *consecrated* Bishop can alone take cognisance, . . . but of those which pertain to simple jurisdiction, a Bishop elected and confirmed, although not yet consecrated, takes cognisance [*Rebuffus de Pacificis possess. n.*243], because the exercise of jurisdiction is acquired by confirmation." [*Barbosa de off. et potest. Episcopi, part* 1, *bk.* 1, *c.* 1. *Edit.* 1560.]

From the above extracts in connection with the argument adduced in Section I., as to the universal jurisdiction of the Episcopate, it is evident that although a Bishop possesses, as of inherent right, universal jurisdiction, yet, for the convenience of ecclesiastical arrangement, this jurisdiction is localised by the assignment to each Bishop of a limited area within which his jurisdiction should be exercised; hence the distinction between *habitual* and *actual* jurisdiction;

the first being expressive of that universal jurisdiction which each Bishop possesses, while the latter, so far from being an augmentation or supplement to habitual jurisdiction, is really a certain form of restriction imposed on it, being, in fact, the limitation of it within a definite area, whether that area be Diocesan, Metropolitan, or Patriarchal, or, as it has been described, "the faculty of exercising jurisdiction in freedom from the intervention of individual Bishops, without prejudice to the paramount authority of the collective Episcopate in Synod"; and the same writer [*Union Review*, 1866] from whom I quote this, gives, as an illustration of the difference between habitual and actual jurisdiction, the position occupied by the judges on circuit. "Every judge is possessed of a real jurisdiction throughout the whole kingdom, which answers to the habitual jurisdiction of the Bishop throughout the Universal Church, but for the time then being exercises this authority, *i.e.*, has actual jurisdiction only on that particular circuit to which he has been for the occasion appointed."

So too "when a Bishop is translated to another see, he does not lose his former *habitual* power of jurisdiction, any more than the sun loses its light when it passes to another hemisphere. When a Bishop is removed from a lesser diocese to a greater, he does not acquire any greater *power*, but only more *subject matter*, to exercise his former power upon. So likewise, when a Bishop is deprived and degraded, he cannot be said to be simply and absolutely deprived of his former power, but the matter is taken away upon which he should exercise his power. This is confessed by Franciscus Vargas, to be the opinion of Alphonsus and others, with whom he himself agrees, and says, 'If it happened, that a Bishop for any crime be deprived of his bishopric, then he shall be deprived of his *subjects*, upon whom he ought to *exercise* his power of jurisdiction, but he shall not be deprived of the power of jurisdiction itself received in his consecration.' [*De Episc. Jurisd.*, *p.* 126.] And Cardinal Cusanus [*de Concord*, *l.* 2, *c.* 13] has determined it exactly in the same manner: 'All Bishops are equal as to their jurisdiction, but not as to the exercise of it; which said exercise is confined and restrained positively within certain bounds, for the greater convenience.'" [*Mason de Minist. Ang.*, *l.* iv., *c.* §, 12.]

But side by side with jurisdiction is the power of mission, and in ascertaining the meaning of this power we are met at once by the difficulty that so many writers have failed to keep clear and distinct the difference between mission and jurisdiction. Sometimes one, sometimes the other, is put for the same thing; and this renders an attempt at explanation a more formidable matter than it otherwise need have been. But going at once to the root of the word, as in the one hand we understand by jurisdiction, the right of declaring the law *a jure dicendo,* and the faculty of any one having public authority over others for their guidance and government; so on the other hand, mission clearly signifies being sent, and is the right by which the power of order is exercised, either as universal mission, by virtue of the Apostolic commission, or in any given place in accordance with Ecclesiastical arrangement. It is, of course, with this latter, as in jurisdiction, with which as a matter of fact we have to do. This definition of the term seems to be the same as that given by Hooker, when he says, "There are but two main things, observed in every Ecclesiastical function—*power* to exercise the duty itself, and some *charge of people,* whereon to exercise the same." [*Eccl. Polity*, *vol.* iii. *p.* 228.] Here clearly the "*power* to exercise the duty itself," is what he otherwise calls the "power of order," while the right to "exercise the same" over "some charge of people" is the mission of which we are speaking.

This distinction is thus illustrated by Rev. Sir W. Palmer, Bart.: "It certainly is essential that the true ministers of God should be able to prove that they have not only the *power* but the *right* of performing sacred offices. There is an evident difference between these things, as may be seen by the following cases:—If a regularly ordained priest should celebrate the Eucharist in the church of another, contrary to the will of that person and of the Bishop, he would have the power of consecrating the Eucharist—it actually would be consecrated; but he would not have the right of consecration, or in other words, he would not have *mission* for that act. If a Bishop should enter the diocese of another Bishop, and contrary to his will ordain one of his deacons to the priesthood, the intruding Bishop would have the *power*, but not the *right*, of ordaining: he would have no mission for such an act. [*Ant. of Eng. Ritual, vol.* ii., *p.* 247; *Oxford,* 1839.]" As a further proof of the importance of mission, if we carry on the argument of Sir W. Palmer a little further, and suppose this missionless priest to be consecrated a Bishop, without having a diocese assigned to him, or one being assigned to him which was full, or which the consecrating Bishops had no canonical right to fill, the result would be that he would be a validly ordained Bishop, but he would have no mission. I mean, of course, no mission in the restricted sense of the word in which we are now using it, in contradistinction to universal mission. Next suppose him to ordain deacons and priests, they would be validly ordained, but would have no mission; or if he were to join other Bishops, similarly situated as himself, in the consecration of a new Bishop, such new Bishop would be validly consecrated, but would have no mission. The force of this (which has already been noticed by the late Mr. Evans, of Baltimore, U.S., in his valuable work on Anglican Ordinations), will appear shortly when the actual case of Archbishop Parker is before us.

Therefore, "in fact, mission fails in all schismatical, heretical, and uncanonical acts, because God cannot have given any man a right to act in opposition to those laws, which He Himself has enacted, or to those which the Apostles and their successors have instituted for the regulation of the Church. He is not the Author of confusion, but of peace, as in all the churches of the saints; and yet, were He to commission His ministers to exercise their offices in whatever places and circumstances they pleased, confusion and division without end must be the inevitable result." [*Ant. of Engl. Rit., vol.* ii., *p.* 248.]

Section III.

It next becomes necessary to examine when this power of jurisdiction is given; but before actually doing so, the following passage from Bishop Gibson [*Introd. to Codex*] is worth careful consideration, as illustrating what has been previously set forth as to the twofold nature of jurisdiction, being exercised—(1) in the *forum externum* of the courts; and (2) in the *forum internum* of conscience and the Sacraments.

"The power" (says Bishop Gibson) "which is vested in the Bishops, for the due administration of government and discipline in the Church of England, appears by the form of consecration to have a twofold original: from the word of God, and from the laws of the land. This is evidently supposed in one of the questions which that form requires every Bishop to answer before the imposition of hands.

'Will you maintain and set forward, as much as shall lie in you, quietness, love, and peace, among all men; and such as be unquiet, disobedient, and criminous within your diocese, correct and punish, according to such authority as you have by God's word, and as to you shall be committed by the ordinance of this realm?'

'Answer.—I will so do, by the help of God.' [*Book of Common Prayer. The Consecration of Bishops.*]

"This plain recognition of the right which the Bishops of the Church of England have to exercise discipline upon the foot of Divine as well as human authority, was in the First Book of Edward VI., and hath ever since continued part of the form of Consecration, and by consequence hath been confirmed by Parliament four several times, viz., by Act of Edward VI., and in three several Acts of Uniformity, whereby the forms of consecration and ordination have been confirmed together with the Book of Common Prayer. . . . . When therefore the laws relating to the royal supremacy, which were made in in the reigns of Henry VIII., Edward VI., and Queen Elizabeth, say that all Ecclesiastical authority is in the Crown and derived from thence, or use any expressions of the like import, it is to be remembered that the principal intent of all such laws and expressions was to exclude the usurped power of the Pope, and that they must be interpreted consistently with that other authority, which our Constitution acknowledges to belong to every Bishop by the word of God. And it is by way of distinction from this, that Judge Hales (speaking of the legal power of Bishops) called it jurisdiction *in foro exteriori*, which is confessed on all hands to be derived from the Crown, viz., the external exercise and administration of justice and discipline in such courts, and in such ways and methods, as are by law or custom established in this realm." [*Gibson, Codex Introd.*]

When then does the Bishop receive that power of jurisdiction which comes to him immediately from God? Here we are met by a difference of opinion, some affirming that it is given in confirmation, others in consecration. "It is the doctrine of our churches, that no man may presume to exercise the various branches of episcopal power and jurisdiction, until 'by public prayer, with imposition of hands,' he be 'approved and admitted thereunto by lawful authority' [*Preface to Ordinal*]; from which we naturally infer that episcopal jurisdiction is conferred by ordination only." [*Palmer, Episcop. Vind., p.* 13.]

Again, "Jurisdiction, according to the Primitive Church, must have been either conferred *in* ordination or *before* it. Let us consider what occurred *before* ordination. When a See became vacant by the death of its Bishop a successor was elected by the clergy and people, and his claim to ordination thus commenced. But was a prelate *merely elect*, and not consecrated, entitled to *exercise jurisdiction?* Certainly not. Such a thing was unheard of in the Primitive Church, and it remains prohibited by the Canon Law, even of the Roman Church, to the present day. [*See Decret. Greg. IX.. lib.* 1, *tit.* 6, *c.* 17; *Van. Espen, Jur. Eccl., p.* 1, *tit.* xiv., *c.* §.] But according to the discipline of the Church for more than a thousand years, election was immediately followed by ordination or consecration: there was no other confirmation of a prelate elect except his consecration." [*Episc. Vind., pp.* 18, 19.] Upon this point Van Espen remarks—"In the early discipline, which remained unshaken for ten centuries, the confirmation of Bishops was scarcely separated from their consecration, but the Bishop elect, having been examined by the Metropolitan and Comprovincial Bishops, was consecrated and confirmed as it were by one and the same act; or rather they confirmed him by ordaining him; neither before ordination was he called Prelate or Bishop, at least not without the addition of elect. Moreover, from the letter of the Decretals, as, amongst others, Fagnanus remarks in the chapter '*Eam te tit. de Rescriptis,*' before consecration he is not called a Bishop simply, but *elect,* 'and with reason,' says he, 'for election and consecration make a Bishop. . . . . 'There,' says Thomassinus [*de Disciplina Eccl., part* 4, *lib.* 2, *c.* 50, *num.* 3,] 'are the remains of the early discipline which did not separate confirmation from consecration, in truth amongst the early writers before the tenth or eleventh century there is scarcely any mention made of confirmation of Bishops, but election, consecration, and ordination only.'" [*Van Espen, Jur. Eccl., part* 1, *tit.* 14, *c.* 4, §§ 1, 2.] See also on this subject De Marca [*De Concord. Sac. et Imp., l.* vi., *c.* 3, *sect.* 8.] "Therefore," concludes the writer before quoted, "jurisdiction, according to the Primitive Church, is not given by election, it is possessed immediately after ordination; therefore it must be given in ordination, because nothing else intervened between election and ordination." [*Episc. Vind., p.* 20.]

On the other hand we find Bishop Gibson writing thus—"After election and confirmation (and not before) the Bishop is fully invested with a right to exercise all spiritual jurisdiction. So saith J. de Athon, 'Although one elected in this manner acquires full authority (*plenum jus*) by canonical election, yet the exercise of that authority he hath not before confirmation.' And Lyndwood wrote, 'And here remember that under the title of Bishop, in matters of jurisdiction, is understood one confirmed, although not consecrated.' Accordingly the sentence of confirmation at this day, conveys in form the care, government, and administration of spirituals; and by Canon Law the Bishop elect, etc., before confirmation is forbidden to intermeddle in the administration of spirituals or temporals. . . . . The books *of Common Law* differ much in their opinions and declarations concerning the commencement of the jurisdiction of a Bishop; some holding that the power of the guardian of the spiritualities ceases (and by consequence that the power of the Bishop commences) upon election; others that he hath no right to exercise any manner of jurisdiction until after confirmation; and others again choose a third way, that his jurisdiction as to all ministerial acts (certificates of bastardy and the like) commences upon election, but as to judicial acts, not till after confirmation; but in those who will have it commence at election, it seems a fair and natural interpretation, that by election they mean election completed by confirmation, and then the next step is consecration; that election is an incomplete act, which may by many ways be undone; that by it a Bishop gains neither jurisdiction nor order, the first of which he hath by confirmation, the second by consecration, the power remains to the guardian of the spiritualities to execute both ministerial and judicial acts, till the Bishop by confirmation is rendered capable to do the same." [*Gibson, Codex, vol.* 1, *p.* 132.]

I have stated the arguments on both sides thus at length, because, as is often the case, the truth lies somewhere between the two. It is true that a Bishop elected and confirmed does enter upon the right of exercising certain acts of jurisdiction, such as I have already shewn, p. 12, for immediately upon the vacancy of a See, the Dean and Chapter enter upon the exercise of certain acts of jurisdiction: hence the jurisdiction entered upon by the Bishop at his confirmation (or more strictly his election completed by confirmation) is that of the Chapter, while into the full power of jurisdiction he enters only at his consecration. And here it is well to note, as a reference to the act of confirmation would show, that confirmation is not a distinct act intermediate between election and consecration, but simply the completion of election, for it is not the *person* elected, but the *election* of the person that is confirmed. So De Marca says, "To the clergy of the city with the consent of the people was assigned the election of the future Bishop, and to the cognisance of the Metropolitans, together with the Bishops of their province, was reserved the rejection or confirmation of the decree passed concerning the election." [*De Concordia, lib.* viii., *c.* 2, § 1.] As to the jurisdiction entered upon by the Dean and Chapter *sede vacante*, we find it set forth as follows by Van Espen, "Hence from the tradition of the Fathers is handed down to us that upon the Cathedral Chapter, as representing the clergy of the Church, devolves the government of the diocese and the Episcopal authority itself, during the vacancy of a see, *cap.* 11 *and* 14, *tit. De Majorit., et obed. cap. unico, Ne sede vacante in* vi., *cap. penult. ae suppl. neglig. Prælatorum in* vi., and from many other passages from which canonists draw this rule: The Chapter, *sede vacante*, performs the office of the Bishop, and succeeds to all things which belong to ordinary jurisdiction, cases expressed in law being excepted, although even they belonged not to the Bishop *jure communi*, but only by custom, or statute or special permission; provided only they belong to him as Bishop and Ordinary.

"But Cardinal Luca rightly remarks [*Disc.* 31, *in Conc. Trid.*], 'that during the vacancy of the Episcopal See, the Episcopal jurisdiction, and administration of the Church devolves on the Chapter *de jure*, not indeed by some privilege or delegation, but by reason *juris non decrescendi;* because the Cathedral Church is composed of the Bishop and Chapter *conjunctim;* of the former truly as the head, of the latter as the body; the Ecclesiastical jurisdiction residing *habitually* in the *whole* body; but its exercise commonly in a competent head!' Hence he infers, N. 3, 'And consequently, the head being removed, all the jurisdiction, or all the *jus Cathedraticum*, both habitual as well as actual, by right of consolidation, or by right *non decrescendi*, remains in the Chapter, as the remaining bodily politic, or intellectual.' Wherefore these things which belong to Bishops, by right of their Episcopal jurisdiction, belong *sede vacante* to the Chapter, unless, as has been said already, they are excepted by special law." [*Van Espen; Jur. Eccl. Univ., pars.* I., *tit.* ix., c. 1, §§ 2, 3, 4.

"The Chapter, *sede vacante*, succeeds the Bishop as ordinary pastor and judge of all his Church, and in all things, which belong to him as *Bishop*, supplies his place, unless they are specially excepted; but those things which are attributed to the Bishop, *not as Bishop* or *Ordinary* of his Diocese, but in another *special* quality, and, *as it were, an extraneous one*, in these the Chapter does not represent the Bishop, nor supply his place." [*Ibid, c.* 11, § 1.]

To this general summary may be added—Collation to benefices, confirmation or institution upon the presentation of a patron, either lay or clerical, or in the case of collation belonging both to the Bishop and Chapter *conjunctim.* But seeing that those things which belong to Episcopal order depend on Episcopal character, which is communicated neither to the Chapter nor to any one of the Chapter, this power of conferring orders does not pass on to the Chapter, but it can give license for any of its subjects to receive orders in another diocese.

Further, within eight days after the death of the Bishop, an Official, or vicar-general, must be appointed by the Chapter, from whom he receives jurisdiction; or, as sometimes was the case, to the Official was entrusted the exercise of contentious, and to the vicar-general that of voluntary jurisdiction, the offices being regarded as distinct, and held by separate persons.

It is this jurisdiction exercised by the Chapter, or its nominee, which is conferred upon the Bishop when his election by the Chapter is completed by his confirmation, which last act also puts an end to the vacancy of the See: and in accordance with this, "before consecration a Bishop cannot exercise those things which belong to order, but only those which belong to jurisdiction. A Bishop receives jurisdiction in confirmation, even before consecration; whence a Bishop confirmed, although not yet consecrated, can excommunicate, suspend, interdict, visit, correct, punish, convoke a synod, confer benefices, unite lesser churches, annex, divide, relax the obligation of a vow and an oath, reserve to himself absolution of certain sins, and such like." [*Ferraris, Promta Bibliotheca.*]

That a Bishop receives jurisdiction in consecration is clear from the ancient forms for consecrating Bishops, *e.g.* in the Sacramentary of Gelasius, the Church prays thus on behalf of the elect: "Give him, O Lord, the keys of the kingdom of heaven; that he may make use of, not glory in, the power which Thou givest for edification, not for destruction. . . . Give unto him the episcopal throne to govern Thy Church and universal people." In the Roman

Pontifical the same words, "Give him, etc.," are found in the prayer of consecration, that the Bishop elect may receive the power of jurisdiction, and afterwards when the pastoral staff is given, "Receive the staff of thy Pastoral Office; that in correcting vices thou mayest be rightly fierce, holding judgment without wrath," etc.; and at the delivery of the Gospels, "Take the Holy Gospel, and go, preach to the people committed unto thee." The English Church likewise confers not only the ministerial function in general, but the ministration of discipline also in particular, that is to say, the power of jurisdiction, by the means of consecration, for the person to be consecrated is presented to the Archbishop by two Bishops in these words—"Most Reverend Father in God, we present unto you this godly and well learned man to be ordained and consecrated Bishop." Shortly after the Archbishop and Bishops present lay their hands upon him, the Archbishop saying, "Receive the Holy Spirit," that is, such ghostly and spiritual power, or grace of the Holy Spirit, as is requisite to this end, to advance a Priest to the office of a Bishop. So that in these words is given to the new Bishop whatsoever appertains to the Episcopal Office, as the prayers preceding this imposition of hands, as well as those following, manifestly declare, in which we humbly beseech Almighty God, "Grant to this Thy servant such grace, that he may evermore be ready to spread abroad Thy Gospel, the glad tidings . . . and use the authority given him, not to destruction, but to salvation, not to hurt, but to help," and afterwards the Archbishop delivers the Bible to him saying . . . "So minister discipline, that you forget not mercy."

"Wherefore, when S. Paul doth put Timothy in remembrance to stir up the grace which was in him by the laying on of hands [2 *Tim.* i. 6] he does not [according to Salmeron's interpretation] confer the gift of order only, but that of jurisdiction also: and when S. Ambrose says 'that God giveth the grace,' [*de Dignit. Sacerdot., cap.* 5,] he undoubtedly means all episcopal grace. For who can give grace to the Pastors of the Church but only the God of all grace, who raises up Pastors to His Church, and makes them rulers over His household? To Salmeron we may add Henricus Gandavensis, who affirms, 'that Bishops have their power, both of order and jurisdiction, immediately from Christ;' as also Gottifridus de Fontibus, and Johannes a Poliaco; all cited by Salmeron, whose opinions he censures without reason, since they had in effect affirmed the whole thing a little before. But the University of Paris speaks clearly enough upon this noted question, where they say 'It is consonant to Evangelical and Apostolical truth, to say, that the power of jurisdiction of the lower prelates, whether they be Bishops or Curates, is derived immediately from God.' [*Decr. Sacr. Facul. Theolog. Paris, prop.* 6.] Moreover, that famous University ordered one Johannes Sarazim, who had taught the contrary, to make his recantation thereof. . . . So likewise, when a Bishop is deprived and degraded, he cannot be said to be simply and absolutely deprived of his former power, but the matter is taken away upon which he should exercise his power. This is admitted by Franciscus Vargas, to be the opinion of Alphonsus, and others as well as his own. Cardinal Cusanus also has determined it exactly in the same manner: 'all Bishops,' says he, 'are equal as to their jurisdiction, but not as to the exercise of it; which said exercise is confined and restrained positively within certain bounds for the greater convenience.' [*De Concord, bk.* 2, *c.* 13.]" [*Mason, Vind., bk.* 4, *c.* 1.]

From this we conclude "that the universal jurisdiction which inheres in the Episcopal Office, and that special limitation of its ordinary exercise to a particular district, commonly called actual jurisdiction over a specific diocese, are conferred, the one in and by consecration in the abstract, the other in and by consecration to a specific See in particular, whenever such consecration takes place." [*Union Review*, 1866.]

But side by side with this jurisdiction which conferred in consecration flows directly from God, is that which Judge Hales, as quoted above, p. 17, calls "jurisdiction *in Foro Exteriori;* which is confessed on all hands to be derived from the Crown, viz., the external exercise and administration of justice and discipline in such courts, and in such ways and methods, as are by law or custom established in this realm."

In examining how far this jurisdiction flowing from the Crown is consonant with the teaching of the Church, I do not purpose to enter (more than incidentally) upon the question of the Royal Supremacy and the present appellate jurisdiction, because the first embraces in reality a wider range than is necessarily involved in an examination of episcopal jurisdiction; while as to the second, the sincere prayer of every churchman must be that the present Court of Appeal, "The Judicial Committee of the Privy Council," may as speedily as possible be amended, and the true right and privilege of the Church, that "Ecclesiastical causes should be handled by Ecclesiastical persons," restored to her again, so that pending the appeal from the decision of a Bishop to that of the Archbishop, and from that of the Archbishop to the Sovereign of the realm, yet the trial should, by order of the Sovereign, be decided with, at least, the assistance of ecclesiastical judges, a principle in itself one of the charters of the Church, as laid down again and again, notably in the Constitutions of Clarendon, A.D. 1164, by the 8th of which it was declared that appeals lay from the "Archdeacon to the Bishop; from the Bishop to the Archbishop; and thirdly, if the Archbishop failed to do justice, recourse may be had to the king, by whose order the controversy was to be decided in the Archbishop's Court:" for as the Establishment is part Canon and part Statute law, so the Court should be part Bishops and part Judges.

Every Bishop, then, receives from the Crown that external coercitive jurisdiction through and by means of which the spiritual is supported and enforced by the temporal power; and Mason thus expresses it:—"Though a Bishop, *as Bishop*, can only use the spiritual sword, yet it is sometimes expedient that there should be some *civil* power annexed to the Episcopal order, to compel and restrain for temporal punishments externally, ... but this coercive power which inflicts temporal punishments, is wholly derived from the king." [*De Minist., lib.* iv., *c.* 1.] Therefore it is that in this power of external jurisdiction the spirituality and the temporality must be treated as united. The Church, *e.g.*, excommunicated Paul of Samosata, but upon his refusal to obey the spiritual censure, the civil power of the Emperor was appealed to, which at once lent its aid to turn him out of the Church and clergy house. It is this power of coercitive jurisdiction exercised by the Sovereign through the Bishops which the Church admits in the oath of supremacy: in which all that is affirmed, is, that the "Sovereign of England, like her predecessors, and all other Christian kings and emperors, has the right from ancient custom, universal consent of the Church, and expediency, to direct, control, and support the affairs of the Church in this empire, for its own good, and according to the law of God and the canons; while at the same time it permits us to add, that there are pastors, who have a Divine right to administer spiritual affairs; that the Sovereign cannot invade their peculiar office; and can do nothing lawfully against the Christian faith and discipline, the canons, or the benefit of the Church." [*Palmer, Ant. of Anc. Rit., vol.* 1, *p.* 277.]

Every student of ecclesiastical history is aware that from a very early age, from the time in fact that the State became Christian, this joint exercise of the temporal and spiritual powers has ever existed, although it bore within itself, by reason of encroachments on the one side or the other, the seed of many a quarrel. As in the early Jewish Church the kings of Israel and Judah exercised authority in ecclesiastical affairs, so Christian emperors and kings have restrained with the civil sword an undue exercise of the power of the clergy; and while they supported them in what was their right, so also did they enforce the ecclesiastical canons, and with the consent and advice of the Bishops made new laws and regulations for the external and internal benefit of the Church.

This concordat between the sacerdotal and imperial power has been set forth by the learned Archbishop de Marca in his well-known work, "*De Concordia Sacerdotii et Imperii,*" from which, in quitting this portion of our subject, I shall venture to extract a few passages.

"Truly that no spiritual authority was in the power of princes, is admitted by all, since Christ committed the power of binding and loosing and the care of feeding the flock to Peter and the Apostles, and to those whom they should make partakers of this ministry. . . . . Certainly because, on the other hand, it may be affirmed, that in the first ages of the Church the supreme power was in the hands of unbelievers, who being enemies to the faith, it is no wonder that the care of ruling the Church was not entrusted to them; but when kings became the nursing fathers of the Christian Church, as Isaiah had prophesied, a notable wrong would be done to Christian princes, if we should refuse them that power in the Church which the kings of the Jews possessed in the synagogue." [*De Marca, de Concord., lib.* ii., *c.* iv., §§ 2, 3. *Edit.* 1788.]

"Although to put forth laws concerning ecclesiastical and spiritual matters is not contained within the limits of royal authority, as I have explained in the seventh chapter; yet by virtue of their office princes are held to preserve canonical constitutions by their laws. Which I should wish to be understood thus, that princes not only when entreated and asked should give their help for the observance of Canons, but also by virtue of their office devote themselves to this charge. . . . . .

"To this duty (*the promoting the good of the State and the happiness of each individual member of it*) the Emperor Theodosius confessed himself bound, in that letter which he wrote to the Council at Ephesus. . . . . From this it is clear, that a certain alliance and relationship existed between religion and the State; to the care of the prince pertained equally the State ecclesiastical as the peace of the empire; that it was the king's duty to keep it firm and inviolate by the consent of all, to preserve sincerity of piety and religion, and to take care that the lives of those who belonged to the clergy should be chastened and pure. . . . .

"Now this duty of guarding the Church was committed to Christian princes by Christ Himself, as we learn on the authority of the Fathers taken from Holy Scripture. On this the Apostle Paul teaches us, that it had been received from God, that kings should be brought to the Christian faith, and that being made Christians should retain their royal dignity; so that, their want of faith being cast aside, they should show forth to other Christians a quiet life united with piety and holiness. For this seems the true meaning of these words: 'I exhort therefore that, first of all, supplications, prayers, intercessions, and giving of thanks, be made for all men: for kings and for all that are in authority;

that we may lead a quiet and peaceable life in all godliness and honesty. For this is good and acceptable in the sight of God our Saviour; who will have all men to be saved, and to come unto the knowledge of the truth.' [1 *Tim.* ii. 1—4.] For this duty kings cannot discharge unless they retain their own authority and the power of the sword, which God gave them. . . . . .

"Wherefore Pope Leo did not hesitate to address the Emperor Leo in these words: 'You must remember, without doubt, that the royal authority is committed to you not alone for the government of the world, but also especially for the protection of the Church; so that by repressing wicked attempts, you may both defend those things well appointed, and restore peace to those which have been disturbed.'" [*Leo, Epist.* 81. *De Marca, de Concord., lib.* ii., *c.* x., §§ 1, 3, 4, 6.]

These passages, which could be multiplied at pleasure, afford abundant proof that the authority vested in Christian Sovereigns was to be exercised, not only in the temporal affairs of their kingdoms, but in spiritual ones also; and, therefore, as in temporal matters, the authority of the king is delegated to civil judges and officers who exercise that authority in the name of the king, by virtue of the power of jurisdiction committed to them on their appointment to their offices, and which is exercised *in foro exteriori* of the courts, not *in foro interiori* of the conscience; so in spiritual matters, this same authority, which the king, as supreme governor of the state, exercises over all his subjects, is delegated by him to officers *in spiritualibus*, that is, to the Bishops of the Church; so that the discipline of the Church is enforced and supported, and a jurisdiction which they, equally with the officers of the state, receive from him, is exercised *in foro exteriori* by those who are the executors of that ecclesiastical supremacy which he holds as Sovereign of the realm, which supremacy may be briefly summed up as follows:—"He (the king) is to *defend the faith* of the Catholic Church, and, therefore, to repress all attempts to introduce heresies and errors. He is *to enforce and execute the discipline* of the Church, and to prevent any of its members from resisting the spiritual powers constituted by Jesus Christ. He is to preserve the peace and unity of the Church, procuring the termination or suppression of controversies. He is to see that *the ministers of the Church fulfil the office of their vocation*; that *ecclesiastical tribunals* do not themselves transgress *the laws of the Church*; that *abuses and imperfections injurious to the efficiency of the Church* be removed.

"In effecting these objects, he is to act in such a manner as does not violate the essential characteristics of the Church. He is invested with the power of summoning synods to deliberate on the affairs of the Church, and to judge questions of doctrine. He has the right of making injunctions or ecclesiastical laws confirmatory of the Catholic doctrine and discipline, with the advice of competent persons; and he may enforce his decrees, not by the spiritual penalty of excommunication, but by temporal penalties." [*Palmer, On the Church, vol.* ii., *p.*245. *Edit.*1842.]

It is to be observed that the line of argument which has been adopted proceeds upon the general fact of the constitution of Church and State as it now exists in the world, and has existed since the time of the State becoming Christian, under Constantine, and not upon any ideal theory of what the Church would be, existing independently of the State: for, as such a condition, except in the very earliest ages, has never existed at all, it would be unnecessary in examining the question of Episcopal jurisdiction under a certain condition to theorise upon what it would be were that certain condition altered. For instance, as a matter of fact, each Christian kingdom is parcelled out into civil and ecclesiastical divisions, which latter are known by the names of provinces, presided over by Metropolitans, and these again into dioceses, presided over by Bishops, and still further into parishes, presided over by Rectors or Vicars. These divisions and sub-divisions, then, being simply matters of convenient arrangement for localisation of authority and government, and as devised by man capable of change, which change must come upon them, if it come at all, from the same source which originally devised them, viz., the sovereign power; so in treating of ecclesiastical jurisdiction we do so in reference not only to its own universal power but also to these localised divisions; and, therefore, the term Bishop implies, as a matter of practice, the possession of a spot assigned to him by the highest authority in the land possessing the power to do so, and our conception and understanding of the power and authority of a Bishop is dependent upon this; and, therefore, it is unnecessary for our purpose in carrying out our examination of the source and extent of this power and authority to enter upon any theoretical disquisition upon what would be the case were Church and State disunited, and the economy of ecclesiastical divisions broken up, and the kingdom re-parcelled out into new divisions and sub-divisions. All that is needful to bear in mind is, that all the power and all the authority which belong to the Episcopal office as a matter of *Divine right*, and as flowing from God Himself, would remain unchanged; that which would be changed would be that right of exercising his power and authority which a Bishop receives *from man*, *i.e.*, the State, as represented by the Sovereign.

We have next to examine how and whence our Bishops derive their right to exercise local mission.

Mission in general has been already (p. 14) defined as "the right to exercise the power of order;" and this right, as regards universal mission, is inherent in all Bishops by virtue of their apostolic commission, dependant upon the words of Christ Himself: "Go ye into all the world, and preach the Gospel to every creature." Now, this original grant of mission to the Apostolic College, besides being universal, "was also joint, and authorised each of them to teach and administer the sacraments all over the world: but the Apostles themselves instituted dioceses, in which they settled Bishops, giving them the charge of the souls of men within their respective dioceses. It followed that they had authority to determine whom they would employ as their assistants in the work for which they were responsible. These men had a local mission. They had a personal right to exercise the power of order, however and whenever received; but now, when they were allotted to a particular diocese, they were *sent* to that diocese, and had there a particular local mission, which from its nature was exclusive." [*Evans, Essays on Ang. Ordinations, vol.* ii., *p.* 297.]

Mission, *then*, or the right to exercise the power of

order, is given in valid consecration; in fact, ordination is the living spring whence mission flows, as from a fountain. Accordingly, in a settled state of the Church, in which it is divided into dioceses and parishes, it is not easy to find any person who has a right to exercise the power of order, who has not local mission somewhere; and, therefore, we are right in contending that "mission is conveyed in ordination, unless there be some impediment, because the right to use a power is ordinarily conveyed in the grant of the power, and to say otherwise is a mere absurdity." As in the case of a Priest, at his ordination he receives the power of order, and then, either by license of the Bishop proceeds to exercise that power on the spot to which he is sent, or else by presentation, induction, or collation to a vacant living, receives the right to exercise that power in the same way from the Bishop from whom he has received the power itself, or from some other Bishop, who in that case represents to him the Bishop from whom he originally received his ordination; so in the case of a Priest consecrated Bishop, the act of consecration usually pre-supposes the fact of nomination to a vacant See; and, therefore, by receiving the power he receives also, at the same time, the right to exercise that power in a certain place; but in the case of a Bishop translated to another diocese, he possesses, of course, the power of order and the right of universal mission, as well as local or territorial mission in his original See. This last right he must relinquish before he can proceed to his new See; and in this case he cannot receive new mission by consecration, but by some other act, viz., confirmation: "When the lawfulness of his election and his fitness for the place to which he is elected, and his acceptance of his election, have all been formally ascertained by that act." And this has been set forth, as it concerns a Bishop, by Van Espen, as follows:—"According to the ancient and still continued discipline of the Church, all Bishops are, at their ordination, deputed to certain churches, in which they should actually exercise the Episcopal office, from which particular deputation and appointment the necessity of Bishops residing at their churches very plainly arises." [*Jur. Ecc. Univ.*, *p.* 1, *tit.* xvi., *c.* 8, § 1.]

The same writer confirms what has been stated respecting

the mission of Bishops when he says, "Christ the Lord being about to ascend to the Father, and visibly leave the Church, said to His Apostles, 'Go ye into all the world, and preach the Gospel to every creature.' Then adds the sacred text, 'And they went forth, and preached everywhere, the Lord working with them, and confirming the word with signs following.'" [*S. Mark* xvi. 20.]

"Christ therefore by no means sent His Apostles to a *fixed* and limited *part* of the world, but into the *whole* world, that they should teach *all* nations, and preach *everywhere*. But as they each could not preach the Gospel, and actually carry on the Apostolic work, *everywhere*, but only in that part of the world in which they were present, in the beginning indeed, by common and mutual consent, and that too not without internal inspiration of the Holy Spirit, because they were few, to spread, as eye-witnesses of the life and doctrine of Christ and His resurrection, the Gospel throughout the whole world; they each chose out somewhat wide, and diffused portions of the world, or as we now say, dioceses; so that each one might have entire and very wide kingdoms as his own diocese, in which each should actually labour (*actu*).

"To these, wheresoever the Apostles came, they not only preached the Gospel, and taught the people, and founded churches, but they also created Bishops especially for them, to whom they entrusted the churches newly founded; and moreover where they themselves were unable to go, having duly instructed disciples in the doctrine of Christ, and ordained them, they sent them away, and that to large dioceses, and with power of appointing and ordaining others.

"An example of this we have in the Apostle Paul, who left Titus at Crete: 'That,' says he, 'thou shouldest set in order (correct) the things that are wanting, and ordain elders in every city, as I had appointed thee,' [*Epist. to Titus, c.* 1]: whose (S. Paul's) former work had confirmed other churches also, as Dalmatia and Corinth. So that it cannot be doubted, that in the time also of the Apostles there were Bishops, who, as the Apostles did, passing indiscriminately through the world, and various countries, spread the *seeds* of the Gospel; but others were appointed and nominated to particular parts of the world or churches; which however made no essential difference between them.

"But after the death of the Apostles, the Church perceiving that from this undivided rule confusion not seldom arose, and disturbance in the government of the Church, 'to each pastor (as S. Cyprian says) was assigned a portion of the flock, which each might rule and govern." And this discipline seemed so necessary for the taking away of confusion, that the Church has preserved it up to this day, and frequently established it by various canons, and strongly forbidden Bishops to regulate anything in another diocese, or to do anything without the licence of the Bishop of that diocese.

'Let not a Bishop go to a strange city which is not subject to him, nor to a country which does not belong to him, for the ordination of any one, or to constitute Priests or Deacons for places subject to another Bishop, unless indeed with the consent of the proper Bishop of the place; but if any shall dare *to do* such a thing, the ordination is null, and he shall receive correction from a Synod.' [*Canon* 22, *Synodi Antiochenæ.*]" [*Van Espen, Jur. Eccl. Univ., pars.* 1, *tit.* 16, *c.* 5, §§ 1—6.]

In conjunction with this canon may also be quoted the thirteenth of the same Council of Antioch, A.D. 341, and the eighth of the third Œcumenical Council of Ephesus, A.D. 431.

"Let no Bishop dare to go from one province into another, and ordain in the Church certain *men* to the honour of the ministry, not even if he bring others with him, unless he come invited by the letters of the Metropolitan, and of the Bishops with him, into whose country he comes. But if, while nobody invites him, he goes forth in a disorderly manner for the ordination of certain persons and the regulation of ecclesiastical matters which belong not to him, the things that have been done by him indeed are null, and he also is to suffer the proper punishment for his irregularity and unreasonable attempt, being deposed forthwith by the Synod." [*Canon* 13, *Synodi Antiochenæ; Edit. Lambert.*]

" . . . . And the very same shall be observed also in other dioceses and provinces everywhere, so that none of the Bishops most beloved by God do assume any other province that was not formerly, and from the beginning subject to him, or to his predecessors. But if *any* one have even assumed, and by force have reduced it under him, he must give it up, lest the Canons of the Fathers be transgressed, or the pride of secular authority be surreptitiously introduced under the mask of the sacred function, or we unknowingly by degrees lose the liberty which our Lord Jesus Christ, the Redeemer of all men, hath given to us by His own blood. It has seemed good, therefore, to the holy and general Synod, that to each province be preserved clear and inviolable the rights formerly and from the beginning belonging to it, according to the old prevailing custom. . . . ." [*Canon* 8, *Synodi Ephesinæ; Edit. Lambert.*]

Impediments to the canonical exercise of jurisdiction and mission are of three kinds—1st, That the See is not vacant; 2ndly, That the consecrators themselves have not the power of consecrating; 3rdly, That the Bishop elected is himself a schismatic or an heretic, and so not capable of receiving jurisdiction. But as these objections refer rather to matters of fact than of theory, they will more appropriately be met by the historical facts, which will be referred to presently, with regard to the right of Archbishop Parker and his successors to exercise true jurisdiction, and to possess real mission.

There is in our own case of the Church of England, the additional accusation laid to her charge by the Romanists, that having become schismatic by the rejection of the jurisdiction of the Pope, in the reign of Henry VIII., any exercise of jurisdiction or mission on the part of her Bishops and Priests is null and void. Any argument on this point would necessarily assume the fact that we admit ourselves to be schismatical, which we deny in the fullest sense of the word. If our opponents, as we are unfortunately obliged to regard them, choose to think so, we cannot help it, and the fact that they do think so, apart from the principles of Christian charity, makes very little difference to us; but let them, for the burden of proof is clearly on the side of the accuser, produce any canon of any Œcumenical Council, which gives to the Pope the right of jurisdiction over the Church of England: this they cannot do, to say nothing of the additional fact which Ecclesiastical history supplies, *ex abundantiâ*, that this claim to exercise jurisdiction on the part of the Pope has been constantly and strenuously resisted. And there is this further fact to be borne in mind, that the rejection of the Pope's jurisdiction in England was the act of the State, which, by virtue of its own authority, cast off a yoke which had now become intolerable; and the Acts of Parliament, which were then passed against the authority of the Pope, all relate to the various branches of ordinary jurisdiction over the Church of England, which the Popes had gradually and illegally acquired, *e.g.*, the payment of annates, the issuing of bulls, right of appeals and dispensations. As Archbishop Bramhall remarks, "Neither King Henry VIII., nor any of our legislators, did ever endeavour to deprive the Bishop of Rome of the power of the keys, or any part thereof, either the key of order, or the key of jurisdiction—I mean jurisdiction purely spiritual, which hath place only in the inner court of conscience, and over such persons as submit willingly—nor did ever challenge or endeavour to assume unto themselves either the key of order, or the key of jurisdiction, purely spiritual. All which they deprived the Pope of, all which they assumed to themselves, was the external regiment of the Church by coactive power, to be exercised by persons capable of the respective branches of it. This power the Bishops of Rome never had or could have justly over their subjects, but under them whose subjects they were." [*Schism Guarded, p.* 392.] True, the Bishops and clergy concurred with the State in abolishing this usurped jurisdiction; but they had the power to do so, for it was not *jure divino*, and, therefore, their doing so involved no act of schism on their part. Therefore, although as a matter of honour and respect, we might be willing to acknowledge the primacy of the See of Rome, and in a certain sense that it is the centre of unity; yet from that acknowledgment it by no means follows that a refusal to admit that honour and respect constitutes an act of schism; in fact, there is here a great temptation to retort, and to ask whether in reality the act of schism was not on the other side. At all events, the records of Queen Elizabeth's reign afford a very strong evidence as to the fact, for it is certain that although the authority of the Pope was rejected in the reign of Henry VIII., it was not till the eleventh year of the reign of Queen Elizabeth that any real division of the two communions took place; until that date (1570), except during the schismatical proceedings under Mary, all the people were subject to the same pastors, attended the same churches, and received the same Sacraments. For the truth of this we have the authority of Lord Chief Justice Coke, who says that "generally all the Papists in this kingdom, not any of them did refuse to come to our Church and yield their obedience to the laws established. And thus they all continued, not any one refusing to come to our churches during the first ten years of Her Majesty's government." [*Speech and Charge at Norwich Assizes*, 1607.] And this is further proved by the Queen's own instructions to Walsingham, her resident at the French Court (August 11, 1570), in which, speaking of the leaders of the Roman party, she says, "They did ordinarily resort, from the beginning of her reign, in all open places, to the churches, and to Divine service in the church, without any contradiction or show of misliking." [*Heylin's History of Presbyt., p.* 260.]

This would hardly have been the case had the attending the churches involved the guilt of countenancing the sin of schism. Of course the right of acting as they thought fit was taken from them when Pius IV. deposed the Queen, and excommunicated her and all her adherents.

Into this question, however, we need not further enter, but pass on to another branch of our subject, gathering up the substance of what has been said in the words of one whose deep learning and powerful grasp of the whole subject before us, is admitted by all who know his work: "English clergy derive their jurisdiction from their own Bishops, and these from their Bishops who went before them back to the beginning, as every Christian Church whatever derived theirs, without one thought of the Bishop of Rome, for some 1200 years, and as the whole Eastern Church derives hers until this very day." [*Haddan, Apost. Succ. in the Church of England, p.* 282.]

Section IV.

"By the code of the Universal Church, all jurisdiction in the provinces is given by the Metropolitan, but the Metropolitan himself receives his jurisdiction from the provincial Bishops." [*Bishop of Brechin on the Articles, vol.* ii., *art.* 37, *p.* 771.] In accordance with this law I purpose, before entering upon the historical facts relating to the consecration of Archbishop Parker, as Primate and Metropolitan, to examine the rights and authority exercised by Metropolitans in the Primitive Church, and the position and authority possessed by the Metropolitans of England in particular, one result of which will be to remove any difficulty that may be felt respecting the power of the consecrators of Parker to give him canonical jurisdiction; and by shewing how great was the power possessed by each Metropolitan in his own province, and how entirely independent of any other that power was, at least in the early age of the Church, to prove inferentially that the assumed right of the Pope to universal jurisdiction, *jure divino,* was not only contrary to the Canons, but entirely unsupported by the facts of early ecclesiastical history. Respecting the origin of Metropolitans, "it is probable that the Apostles chose cities and towns for their chief ministry, since these were the heart of each country, whence the Gospel would reach most easily to the smaller places. It is in cities where we hear of Apostles abiding; they are cities which, in the main, they address. The metropolis of the country or province became naturally the Ecclesiastical metropolis—the See of the first Bishop of that province. Such grouping of Sees occurs even in the Apostolic Canons. 'The Bishops of each nation must own him who is first among them, and regard him as head, and do nothing extraordinary without his mind.' [*Can.* xxxiii.] The Council of Antioch, making the terms of this more definite, speaks of it as 'the Canon of our Fathers,' and assigns the reason. 'The Bishop in each Eparchy must own the Bishops presiding in the metropolis, and submit to his thought for the whole Eparchy, because in the metropolis all from all sides who have matters meet together; whence it seemed good that he should be first in honour, and that the other Bishops,' etc. [*Can.* ix.] The Council of Laodicea requires that 'the Bishops should be set in their Ecclesiastical rule by the judgment of the Metropolitans, and the Bishops around.' [*Can.* xii.] The Council of Eliberis speaks of 'the place in which the first See of the Episcopate is established.' [*Can.* xxxviii.] The Council of Nice lays down that 'a Bishop should be appointed by all the Bishops in the Eparchy; but if this should be difficult on account of a pressing necessity or length of way, that three should meet together, the absent ones concurring and agreeing by letter, but that the validity of what took place should in each Eparchy be assigned to the Metropolitans.' [*Can.* iv.] It has alike no other title for the highest Sees than 'the Bishop in Rome,' 'the Bishop in Alexandria.' The substance existed without the name." [*Bishop of Brechin on the Articles, vol.* ii., *art.* 37, *pp.* 701, 702.)

These words of Bishop Forbes sum up in a brief compass the position of Metropolitans in the early Church, and this we find borne out by a reference to Van Espen, Thomassinus, De Marca, and other canonists. The former, indeed, (Van Espen) adds to the fourth Nicene Canon, already quoted, the sixth: "This is already manifest, that if any be made a Bishop without the consent of the Metropolitan, the great Synod has determined such an one ought not to be a Bishop."

He then proceeds to show how from one step to another the rights of Metropolitans were obtained, and that that which in the first place was accorded, as a mark of honour and respect, by degrees was demanded as a right: "For as of old it was the custom, that Bishops should be ordained by neighbouring Bishops, or by those of the same province, it easily came to pass, that when by degrees, from the renown of the cities, the dignity of the Bishops received an increase, and access of other Bishops upon various incidental matters was more frequent to the Metropolitan cities, ordinations began to take place in the Metropolis itself, and to be performed by the Bishop who was set over the Metropolis, the other Bishops of the province assisting.

"This, although at the beginning it was an act of free-will, at length passed into an act of necessity; and thus by custom, rather than by any positive decree, the right of ordaining provincial Bishops, claimed in early times by the Metropolitans, was afterwards confirmed by the Canons of the Nicene Council, and declared to be wholly reserved to them. . . . . But after that by degrees these rights of Metropolitans were confirmed, first by the Canon of Nicæa, and then by other Canons, they themselves also began to be called Archbishops, by which name they were not known in the time of S. Leo, that is, in the fifth century, at least amongst the Latins, as the learned Paschasius Quesnellius has observed, in his Notes to the *Ninth Epistle* of S. Leo, and shows in the same place, that those who admit this to be an authentic epistle of S. Leo, maintain together that the word Archbishop has crept into the text instead of Bishop, by the carelessness of the transcriber. Therefore there is no doubt, that the Bishops, whom a future age called Archbishops, were anciently called simply Metropolitans, a name taken from the Metropolis." [*Jur. Eccl. Univ., par.* 1, *tit.* xix.]

We have already shown (p. 36), from the thirty-third of the Apostolic Canons, and the ninth of the Antiochene, what was the position of Metropolitans towards their Suffragans: "From these it is clear, that the government or direction of their dioceses was free to each Bishop, neither were the Metropolitans allowed to disturb this government; yet the Bishops were to recognise the Metropolitan as *head* and superior, who, according to the rules laid down for him by the Church, could, either alone or together with the other comprovincial Bishops, correct, and sometimes punish delinquents, or those who, in the government of their dioceses, departed from the rules prescribed by the Canons, and in that sense the Metropolitan was now long since regarded as ordinary admonisher, corrector and judge of his Suffragans. . . . . .

"But there is nothing which more clearly expresses the obedience and subjection which from long since Bishops owed to their Metropolitans than the oath which they were bound to take at their ordination, the form of which is still preserved in the Pontifical under the title *De Scrutinio Serotino.*

"*Under this title* is described by what rite the examination of the Bishop and his consecration are performed by the Metropolitan; so that while the election itself of the Bishops was in the hands of the cathedral Canons, both the confirmation and consecration were performed by the Metropolitan; and amongst other things is given the oath to be taken to the Metropolitan by him who is to be ordained. *(Then follows the oath.)* . . . .

"If any one should compare this form with that of the oath which Bishops take to the Roman Pontiff, it will be seen that the Bishops swore the same obedience to their Metropolitans as they now do to the Roman Pontiff." [*Van Espen, Jur. Eccl., pars* 1, *tit.* xix., *c.* 3.]

It is unnecessary for our present purpose to follow the learned canonist any further with regard to the right of Metropolitans to obedience from their Suffragans, otherwise it would have been interesting to have quoted his denunciations upon the forged Isidorian decretals, to which he attributes all the assumed authority of the Popes in after ages; my object is rather to summarise what has been written by others, and with this view I again resort to the same writer for information as to the powers possessed by Metropolitans.

Quoting the seventh Canon of the third Council of Carthage, he says:—" 'Whatever Bishop is accused, let the accuser bring the cause before the Primate of his province, nor let him be suspended from communion, against whom a charge is brought, before he shall at least, summoned by letters from the Primate, have pleaded his cause, on a day appointed.'

"To understand this Canon, it is to be observed that in Africa the Primates of the Provinces were the same as those who are now called Metropolitans; so for Bishops to be accused before the Primate of a Province is the same as to be accused before the Metropolitan." [*Jur. Eccl., pars* 1, *tit.* xix., *c.* 4.]

This ordinary and judicial authority of Metropolitans over their Suffragans he proceeds to prove by canons from various Councils, and a decree of Honorius III., and adds: "Hence with one consent canonists most clearly grant, that *de jure communi* the Metropolitan was the judge ordinary of his Suffragans, and that charges against them could be laid before the Metropolitan by accusation alone, even without appeal; and that the Metropolitans themselves could, upon just cause, inflict certain censures upon their Suffragans." [*Jur. Eccl. Univ.*, p. 1, tit. xix. c. 4, §§ 2—4.]

I have already shewn that to each Bishop his own diocese was assigned, which he should rule with full authority; so that no prelate, without his consent, could exercise any, even the smallest, act of jurisdiction: for, as the Ninth Canon of the Council of Antioch states, "Every Bishop has power over his own diocese, both to regulate it according to the piety which becomes each, and to undertake the care of the whole region subject to his city." "And although the Metropolitan or Archbishop possesses a certain jurisdiction and superiority over his Suffragans, still it is not allowed him to have any *immediate* jurisdiction over the subjects of any of his Suffragans and his diocese.

"Hence canonists commonly hand down, that the Metropolitan indeed is judge of the whole province as having Archiepiscopal jurisdiction, but not as having Episcopal or ordinary jurisdiction over the whole province or each of its dioceses. For Archiepiscopal jurisdiction extends only to his Suffragan Bishops; by no means to their subjects, except *mediately;* as far certainly as the negligence or defect of the Suffragans has to be supplied, or their mode of procedure to be corrected.

"Wherefore the authority of Metropolitans does not extend to the Dioceses of Suffragans, unless the Bishops themselves turn aside from the sacred Canons, or are defective in their execution; so that of Metropolitans may be said that which S. Gregory said of the Apostolic See [*lib.* 7, *epist.* 64, *ind.* 4]: 'If any fault is discovered in Bishops, I know not who is not subject to the Apostolic See; but when a fault does not require it, all by the rule of humility are equal.'

"Therefore the Metropolitan has no ordinary and Episcopal authority, nor can exercise any in the dioceses of his Suffragans, but possesses Archiepiscopal jurisdiction so far as to be able to inquire into the defects of his Suffragans, and correct and supply them.

"For this cause, the Metropolitan, *jure communi,* can

exercise the office of visitation throughout the whole province, or a part of it, by freely visiting cities, dioceses, his Suffragans and their subjects, Chapters of Cathedrals and other churches, monasteries, churches and other religious and pious places, clergy and people, and receive procurations from places visited......

"Moreover, the Metropolitans, as superiors of their Suffragans, may summon their Suffragans to them; and in many Churches it has become customary for Suffragans, at times appointed, to be obliged to present themselves to their Metropolitans. Therefore Metropolitans remain the superiors of the Suffragans, and retain throughout the whole province a Metropolitan authority; so that they supply the defects of Suffragans, and admonish them of their duty, and compel them to execute those things which belong to their office." [*Jur. Eccl. Univ., pars.* 1, *tit.* xix., *c.* 5.]

As the Archbishop or Metropolitan possesses no ordinary jurisdiction in the dioceses of his Suffragans, so, without the consent of the Ordinary, he is unable to perform Pontifical acts, with the exception of visitation; and under the exercise of Pontifical acts the Council of Trent includes not only conferring of orders, but other acts which require some jurisdiction or Episcopal or Pontifical authority. Whence many persons hold that he is not allowed to say Mass in Pontifical vestments without the licence of the Ordinary; and Cardinal de Luca adds, that he may not wear a mozzetta or give the benediction, because that public solemn use of Pontifical ornaments bears some kind of jurisdiction in its exercise. As also the special mark of Archbishops or Metropolitans is the cross, which they cause to be borne before them *elevated*, as a sign of jurisdiction or authority; so, except in the case of visitations, no Archbishop or Metropolitan was permitted to proceed beyond the bounds of his jurisdiction with a cross elevated.

Much that has been quoted from Van Espen will be found to be confirmed by Thomassinus, and therefore will not need to be repeated, but in addition to the authority of the ninth Canon of the Council of Antioch, Thomassinus supplements the rights of the Metropolitans by shewing from Canon xiv. how great was the power of the Metropolitan in *provincial* Synods. "His right it is to convoke them, and to preside over them, inasmuch as in honour and position he excels all the other Bishops of the province. His too, if the suffrages of the comprovincials are divided in a criminal charge against any Bishop, to invite Bishops from the neighbouring provinces, who were to take their seats as judges, and so remove the perplexity. In addition to this, no Bishop deprived of his bishopric could migrate to any other vacant bishopric unless the Council should approve. That moreover is not a true and real council, unless a Metropolitan preside: 'That is a perfect Synod at which the Metropolitan is present.' [*Can.* 16.] Therefore without the authority of the Metropolitan Bishops may not be transferred.

"As often as a new Bishop is to be chosen, it is the duty of the Metropolitan to summon all the Bishops. Twice a year provincial Councils are to be held; it belongs to the Metropolitans to take care, and to see that no Bishop be absent, 'the Metropolitan giving notice of the time to the comprovincials. For it is not permitted to any to convoke Councils, except he do so upon the authority of the Metropolitan:' 'it is not lawful to any to hold Synods by themselves, without those who are intrusted with the metropolis.' [*Can.* 20.]" [*Thomassinus, Vet. et. Nov. Eccl. Discip., pars* 1, *lib.* 1, *c.* xi.]

After continuing his illustration of the rights of Metropolitans by further references to decrees of Councils and Popes, he sums them up briefly as follows: "All causes at least of any importance are to be treated by the Metropolitan and the Bishops of the province; especially in the Council of the province, which he was to convoke, and at which he presided. At a general Council all Metropolitans, by virtue of their office, were to be present. Over the subjects of the Bishops subject to them, they were to exercise jurisdiction, either when an appeal was made to them, or when they visited the province. They were also charged with the duty of seeing the Canons duly observed, and of punishing violations of them. They issued letters of commendation (*litteræ Formatæ*) to Bishops about to travel, and in general manifested their care of all the comprovincial Churches.

"*In the ordination* of Metropolitans themselves they

were to be chosen and consecrated by their own provincial Bishops, and were not obliged to send for a Metropolitan out of another province to do it; but they had power to do it in their own provincial Synod among themselves. This, S. Augustine says, was the custom of the Catholic Church, both in Africa and Rome. And, therefore, when the Donatists objected against Cæcilian, primate of Carthage, 'that his ordination was uncanonical, because he had not sent for the neighbouring primate of Numidia to come and ordain him,' his answer was, 'that Cæcilian had no need of this, since the custom of the Catholic Church was otherwise, which was, not to have the Numidian Bishops to ordain the Bishop of Carthage, but the neighbouring Bishops of the province of Carthage: as it was not the custom at Rome to send for a Metropolitan out of another province to ordain the Bishop of Rome, but he was always ordained by the Bishop of Ostia, a neighbouring Bishop of the same province.' [*S. August. Brevic. Collat.*, 3 *die.*, *c.* 16.]"

Moreover, no Canon is in existence which gives to a Metropolitan the right of ordaining another, neither in ancient times was any Metropolitan obliged to go or send out of his province, much less to Rome, for his ordination; but all was to be done by his Suffragans in his own church.

That this was the practice of the early Church with regard to the election and consecration of Metropolitans, however much that practice has been lost in later ages through the assumptions of the Popes, and the neglect to return to primitive use when the Papal authority was rejected, [although *in theory* the return is made, for the Metropolitan still enters upon his dignity as Metropolitan by the acceptance of the comprovincials,] is confirmed by Peter de Marca, who says, "Undoubtedly the elections and ordinations of Metropolitans were of greater moment than those of other Bishops; and so required greater care. In the elections, the Bishops enjoyed full right of suffrage, and that authority which in the elections of the rest of their colleagues they did not possess; for this reason truly, that as they depended upon the Metropolitan, it was of great importance to them, what kind of man should be called to that *dignity*. Therefore Leo well remarks, 'Upon the death of the Metropolitan, when another is to be chosen into his place, the provincial Bishops must assemble in the metropolitan city, so that the wishes of all the clergy having been discussed, the best one of the Presbyters and Deacons of that Church should be chosen.'" [*De Marca, De Concord, lib.* vi., *cap.* iv.] "Let the Metropolitan Bishop, having been elected by the comprovincial Bishops, clergy, and people, be ordained by the comprovincial Bishops assembled together." [*2nd Council of Aurelia, Can.* 7.]

This is further explained by the third council held at the same place, which sets forth the difference which existed between the elections of Bishops and Metropolitans, and says, "Let the Metropolitan, as contained in the decrees of the Holy See, be chosen by the comprovincial Bishops, with consent of the clergy or people; because it is right, as the Apostolic See itself has said, that he who is to be set over all should be chosen by all. But concerning the ordination of comprovincials with the consent of the Metropolitan, let the election and will of clergy and people, according to the decrees of former statutes, be sought for." [*3rd Council of Aurelia, Can.* 3.]

All that has been advanced respecting the rights and position of Metropolitans in general, applies also to those of the Anglican Church in particular. Admitting the debt of gratitude justly due to S. Gregory, as the author of the mission of S. Augustine to England, still it must not be forgotten (and this is of great importance as regards the claims made in subsequent times of Papal jurisdiction in England) that a Church had existed in England when S. Augustine reached our shores, and that he did not accept the Episcopate as the mere nominee of the Pope, bound to submit to him in all things, but as an independent Bishop of a See in a country which had never been included in the Patriarchate of Rome. Hence, from the words of S. Gregory, when he gave him the pall as a mark of respect and dignity, it will be seen at once that his authority was to be for ever independent of the Apostolic See; that as Primate and Metropolitan he was to be *Autocephalous*. From S. Gregory, by virtue of his inherent universal mission and jurisdiction, which he possessed like every other Bishop, S. Augustine received also universal mission and jurisdiction, conveyed to him by the hands of Vergilius, Archbishop of Arles, who consecrated him, acting as vicar of the Apostolic See. This universal jurisdiction and mission S. Augustine, with the sanction of King Ethelbert, localised by fixing his See at Canterbury, not at London as S. Gregory had directed, probably because of the importance then possessed by the kingdom of Kent among the kingdoms, and Canterbury being the central seat of government; and then proceeded to ordain other Bishops, assigning to each a diocese, with local jurisdiction and mission also. In all this it is to be observed that the state of the case was such that of necessity allowed a relaxation of strict canonical rule. To S. Gregory England was a new mission field: all intercourse between the people of England and the early British Church had ceased; and therefore, although England was in no way subject to his authority, yet by virtue of his universal mission, in sending out a priest of his own for the conversion of the country, his injunctions to him assumed the appearance of an authority which in reality he did not possess, and which, if it had been disallowed by Ethelbert, the sovereign of the kingdom in which S. Augustine fixed his See, could not have been exercised. As it was, Ethelbert, by the influence of his wife Queen Bertha, cordially welcomed the mission, was himself and numbers of his nobles shortly after baptised, and thus the interests of the Church and the State working harmoniously together, the work of evangelisation was allowed to progress without any great let or hindrance.

That the authority was to be afterwards entirely inherent in the English Episcopate without further reference to the Apostolic See, may be gathered from the epistle of S. Gregory to S. Augustine, on the occasion of his sending him the pall. "We grant to you the use of the pall, so that you may ordain twelve Bishops, one to each place, who are to be subject to your authority, since the Bishop of London is for the future to be consecrated by his own Synod, and to receive the pall of honour from this Apostolic See. To York we wish you also to send a Bishop, who may himself also ordain twelve Bishops, and fulfil the office of Metropolitan, for we propose to send the pall to him also, whom we wish to be subject to you, my brother. But after your death let him preside over the Bishops whom he shall have ordained, so that he be in no way subject to the authority of the Bishop of London; but between the Bishops of London and York let there be hereafter this distinction of honour, that he should be regarded as the first who shall have been first ordained."

This injunction was acted upon by S. Augustine, Canterbury being substituted for London; and the line of the Episcopate in England thus founded by him has never been broken, Bishop succeeding Bishop in due canonical order, with all rights of jurisdiction and mission freely attached. And so in tracing this historically, although, as the dimensions of Papal supremacy extended themselves, in proportion to the success which the assumptions met with, these Episcopal rights were to a great extent paralysed by "that jurisdiction which, supported and strengthened by the false decretals, and formularised by individual theologians after the Council of Trent, was for nine hundred years exercised over the Church of England;" yet in theory the authority and jurisdiction of the See of Canterbury was free and independent, only by degrees was submission to Papal authority acquired, and that not without efforts, often successful, to reject it. S. Augustine doubtless was filled with enthusiastic devotion to the See of Rome, whence he had come; but the acts of his successors shew for the most part that in their appeals to Rome for advice or otherwise, it was to one whose superior honour and dignity they reverenced, not to one whose authority and decision they accepted as final.

An example in proof of the authority attached to the See of Canterbury may be seen in the rescript of Pope Gregory to Augustine: "Let your jurisdiction not only extend over the Bishops you shall have ordained, or such as have been ordained by the Bishop of York; but also over all the priests of Britain, by the authority of our Lord Jesus Christ." [*William of Malmesbury, Hist. of the Kings, bk.* iii., *p.* 265.] And still further by the brief of Pope Boniface to Justus, Archbishop of Canterbury: "Far be it from every Christian, that anything concerning the city of Canterbury be diminished or changed in present or future times, which was appointed by our predecessor Pope Gregory, however human circumstances may be changed; but more especially by the authority of S. Peter, the prince of the Apostles, we command and ordain that the city of Canterbury shall ever hereafter be esteemed the Metropolitan See of all Britain. And we decree and appoint immutably, that all the provinces of the kingdom of England shall be subject to the Metropolitan Church of the aforesaid See. And if any one attempt to injure the Church, which is more especially under the power and protection of the Holy Roman Church, or to lessen the jurisdiction conceded to it, may God blot him out of the Book of Life, and let him know that he is bound by the sentence of a curse. (*Anathema.*)" [*William of Malmesbury, Hist. of the Kings of Eng., bk.* iii., *p.* 265, *trans. by Stevenson. Edit.* 1854.]

In both of these Pontifical utterances it is easy to see, notwithstanding the assumed "power and protection of the Roman Church," that a jurisdiction real and active was meant to be given, and to be inherent in the See of Canterbury for ever.

That the occupants of that See, at least up to the time of the Conquest, so regarded it, their history amply testifies: take for example the well-known quarrel for supremacy between the Archbishops of Canterbury and York. An account of it is to be found in detail in Thomassinus [*Vetus et Nov. Eccl. Discip., pars.* 1, *lib.* 1, *c.* 36], from which it appears that on the appointment of Lanfranc to the See of Canterbury, he required from Thomas, Archbishop of York, the usual oath of canonical obedience, enforcing his right by the authority of the king, as well as the consent of the other Bishops. The Archbishop of York obeyed, but in doing so declared that he would not not take the oath to any successor of Lanfranc, unless it should be proved in a Canonical Synod, by what law or right this duty was required of him. Both accordingly set out for Rome, and laid the matter before Pope Alexander II., the Archbishop of York relying upon what he considered a most indubitable authority, viz., the decree of Gregory the Great, by which a friendly equality was assigned to the two Metropolitans of England, so far that he who was ordained first, should have a primacy of honour over the other. To this Lanfranc replied that the decree of Gregory referred to the *status* of the Bishops of *London* and York, and did not mention Canterbury at all, which was certainly the case according to the letter of the decree, S. Augustine himself, as stated above, having fixed the Metropolitan See at Canterbury. The Pope was unable to come to any friendly decision, and referred the matter to a General English Council, to which he sent as his own representative a legate *a latere*.

The Council accordingly was held in 1072, and is thus described by William of Malmesbury :—

"In the year of our Lord Jesus Christ's Incarnation, 1072, of the Pontificate of Pope Alexander, the eleventh, and of the reign of William, glorious King of England, and Duke of Normandy, the sixth; by the command of the said Pope Alexander, and permission of the same King, in presence of himself, his Bishops, and Abbots, the question was agitated concerning the primacy which Lanfranc, Archbishop of Canterbury, claimed in right of his Church over that of York; and concerning the ordination of certain Bishops, of which it was not clearly evident to whom they especially appertained; and at length, after some time, it was proved and shewn by the distinct authority of various writings, that the Church of York ought to be subject to that of Canterbury, and to be obedient to the appointments of its Archbishop, as Primate of all England, in all such matters as pertained to the Christian religion. But the homage of the Bishop of Durham, that is of Lindisfarn, and of all the countries beyond the limits of the Bishop of Litchfield, and the great river Humber, to the farthest boundaries of Scotland, and whatever on this side of the aforesaid river justly pertains to the diocese of the Church of York, the Metropolitan of Canterbury allowed for ever to belong to the Archbishop of York, and his successors; in such sort, however, that if the Archbishop of Canterbury chose to call a a council, wherever he deemed fit, the Archbishop of York was bound to be present at his command, with all his Suffragan Bishops, and be obedient to his canonical injunctions. And Lanfranc the Archbishop proved from the ancient custom of his predecessors, that the Archbishop of York was bound to make profession, even with an oath, to *the Archbishop* of Canterbury; but through regard to the

King, he dispensed with the oath from Thomas, Archbishop of York, and received his written profession only; but not thereby forming a precedent for such of his successors as might choose to exact the oath, together with the profession, from Thomas's successors. If the Archbishop of Canterbury should die, the Archbishop of York shall come to Canterbury, and, with the other Bishops of the Church aforesaid, duly consecrate the person elected, as his lawful Primate. But if the Archbishop of York shall die, his successor, accepting the gift of the Archbishopric from the king, shall come to Canterbury, or where the Archbishop of Canterbury shall appoint, and shall from him receive canonical ordination. To this ordinance consented the King aforesaid, and the Archbishops, Lanfranc of Canterbury, and Thomas of York; and Hubert, sub-deacon of the holy Roman Church, and legate of the aforesaid Pope Alexander; and the other Bishops and Abbots present. This cause was first agitated at the festival of Easter, in the City of Winchester, in the Royal Chapel, situated in the Castle; afterwards in the royal town called Windsor, where it received its termination, in the presence of the King, the Bishops, and Abbots of different orders, who were assembled at the King's Court on the festival of Pentecost. The signature of William the King: the signature of Matilda the Queen. I, Hubert, sub-deacon of the holy Roman Church, and legate from Pope Alexander, have signed. I, Lanfranc, Archbishop of Canterbury, have signed. I, Thomas, Archbishop of York, have signed. I, William, Bishop of London, have assented. I, Herman, Bishop of Shireburn, have signed. I, Wulstan, Bishop of Worcester, have signed. I, Walter, Bishop of Hereford, have signed. I, Giso, Bishop of Wells, have assented. I, Remigius, Bishop of Dorchester, have signed. I, Walkelin, Bishop of Winchester, have signed. I, Herefast, Bishop of Helmham, have signed. I, Stigand, Bishop of Chichester, have assented. I, Siward, Bishop of Rochester, have assented. I, Osbern, Bishop of Exeter, have assented. I, Odo, Bishop of Baieux, and Earl of Kent, have assented. I, Geoffrey, Bishop of Coutances, and one of the nobles of England, have assented. I, Scotland, Abbot of S. Augustine's Monastery, have assented. I, Elfwin, Abbot of the Monastery of Ramsey, have assented. I, Elnoth, Abbot of Glastonbury, have assented. I, Thurston, Abbot of the Monastery which is situate in the Isle of Ely, have assented. I, Wulnoth, Abbot of Chertsey, have assented. I, Elfwin, Abbot of Evesham, have assented. I, Frederic, Abbot of S. Alban's, have assented. I, Gosfrid, Abbot of the Monastery of S. Peter, near London, have assented. I, Baldwin, Abbot of S. Edmund's Monastery, have assented. I, Turold, Abbot of Peterborough, have assented. I, Adelelm, Abbot of Abingdon, have assented. I, Ruald, Abbot of the New-minster at Winchester, have assented." [*William of Malmesbury, Hist. of the Kings, bk.* 3, *pp.* 265, 266.]

Thomassinus also states that Lanfranc informed the Pope by letter of the result of the Council, showing from what took place that it was proved that for a hundred and forty years the Archbishops of Canterbury had exercised the fullest Primatial rights, not only over the See of York, and all England, but also over Ireland; and further, when the decree of Gregory was brought forward, he replied, that in the first place reference was made to London, and not to Canterbury; and next, that the mandate neither was nor could be carried into execution, for at that time there was no Archbishop of York at all, neither was there one until the time of Justus, fourth Archbishop of Canterbury, when Paulinus was nominated to the See of York [A.D. 625], and that as Augustine from the Church of Canterbury, where he had fixed his See, had spread the teaching of Christ throughout all the provinces of England, founded churches, fixed all the Episcopal Sees, the Archbishops of Canterbury were on that account regarded as the authors and founders of them, not only by the English, but also by the Roman Pontiffs who succeeded to the See of Gregory.

These arguments, as already stated, obtained the victory for the See of Canterbury, and a complete vindication of its Primatial rights, and afford another proof that the rights and jurisdiction of the Metropolitan existed, not merely in theory, but in very reality. There is no need to pursue the details of the quarrel further which broke out afresh upon the death of Lanfranc, and the succession of Anselm, and was carried on with great bitterness for many years, ending at length in the right of the Archbishop of York to entitle himself Primate of England, whilst Canterbury was called Primate of all England. Sufficient has been said for our purpose; and if further confirmation were necessary, there is the fact that until the year 1151 Ireland remained under the jurisdiction of Canterbury, and its Bishops received consecration from thence. In that year (in consequence of an application made in 1137 to the See of Rome by S. Malachi, Archbishop of Armagh, for the Pall to be granted to him, and Ireland to be set free from the juris-tion of Canterbury) Eugenius III., after the matter had been considered, granted his request, in spite of the protest of the See of Canterbury, and sent four Palls, the Primacy being subsequently attached to the See of Armagh.

In the Welsh Church, or as it was then called, the British Church, the jurisdiction of the Metropolitan See under S. Augustine was rejected, and the two churches, viz., the British and the English, were divided for a time, *i.e.*, to A.D. 809; yet in A.D. 1095, the claim of Canterbury to Metropolitan jurisdiction was distinctly admitted when Wilfred (or Gryffydd), Bishop of S. David's, was restored (after suspension) by Anselm. This was followed in 1107 by a profession of canonical obedience to the See of Canterbury by Urban, who was consecrated at Canterbury to the See of Llandaff: and from that time, although attempts were made in 1125, and again in 1176, to claim Metropolitanship for S. David's, they were unsuccessful.

So also in the Church of Cornwall was the jurisdiction of Canterbury accepted, for in A.D. 833, or more probably 870, as Professor Stubbs conjectures [*Councils and Ecclesiast. Documents, p.* 674], Kenstec, Bishop of Dinnurrin, "Dingerein," (in Cornwall,) professed canonical obedience to Ceolnoth, Archbishop of Canterbury.

So far then it is clear that the See of Canterbury did possess and exercise Metropolitan jurisdiction, and that the Pope of Rome was voluntarily made the arbiter of any disputes, not as a matter of Divine right, but partly from a feeling of personal affection and gratitude, and partly from respect to his position as Bishop of the first See, and as such to his recognised Primacy. On the other hand, if the authority of the Pope had been exercised *jure divino* to the detriment of the jurisdiction possessed and exercised by both Canterbury and York, we should naturally expect to find that he took a leading part in the confirmation and ordination of Metropolitans; yet the very contrary is the fact, for "till the twelfth century, amongst all the Metropolitans of our churches, only two individuals were consecrated by the Bishop of Rome or his legates. There is not one trace of such ordination in our churches during the ages which elapsed previously to the arrival of Augustine. Pope Gregory did not claim the ordination of that prelate, but wrote to the Archbishop of Arles to consecrate him, and afterwards directed that in all future time the Metropolitans of England should be appointed by their own provincial Synods, as the sacred Canons enjoin. Accordingly out of forty-two Archbishops of Canterbury, from A.D. 597 to A.D. 1138, only two were consecrated by the Bishop of Rome, *i.e.*, Theodore of Tarsus in 668, and Plegmund in 889; the former of whom was only so ordained in a case of absolute necessity. (*The necessity arose from there being at that time only one other Bishop in England; and so, as Bede informs us, Egbert, King of Kent, and Oswi of Northumbria, sent Wigard to Rome to be consecrated Archbishop of Canterbury by Pope Vitaliemus; but he dying at Rome, the Pope named, consecrated, and sent over Theodore in* 668.) Of the twenty-seven Archbishops of York who lived from A.D. 625 to A.D. 1119, *not one* was ordained by the Roman Pontiff or his legates. In the twelfth century, in consequence of disputed elections, which contending parties referred to Rome, the Roman Pontiffs took occasion gradually to usurp the ordination of our Metropolitans; but even in 1162, and in 1234, Thomas à Becket and Edmund Rich were elected and consecrated in England." [*Palmer, Episcop. Vindic., pp.* 125, 126.)

Thomassinus, referring to the Canons of the Aurelian Councils, quoted above (p. 44), and explaining them by reference to the practice of the churches, says, "In these not the slightest trace exists from which it may be supposed that the Metropolitans of Gaul had to be confirmed by the Pope." So again, "the Metropolitans of Gaul were confirmed not by the Pope, but by a provincial Council." *This he proves* by referring to England, where Augustine, having undoubtedly been sent by Gregory to bring over all the island, was directed to create two Metropolitans, of whom the one should confirm the other, and ordered that "the confirmation of the Roman See was not to be waited for." The same rule applied also to the Metropolitans of Spain and of Africa, equally with those of Gaul, and remained unchanged up to the year 800. [*Cf. Thomassinus, Vet. et Nov. Discip., pars* ii., *lib.* ii., *c.* 19.] In point of fact, as Thomassinus shews in c. 43 of the same book ii., it was not until the tenth century that the confirmation and consecration of the Metropolitans and Bishops of the west by the Popes of Rome commenced, and then solely upon the authority of the Isidorian Decretals, and from references being made to them in cases of doubtful or disputed elections; and the cause of it he considers to have arisen in great measure from the cessation of provincial Councils, in consequence of which, appeals began more frequently to be carried to the Popes; for if the Bishops had continued to assemble synodically at the elections of provincial Bishops, and to exercise their rights as chief electors, they would have kept their authority which they were now loosing, and so would have settled all contentions, put an end to strife by their own judgment, consecrated those elected, and have retained their triple power of electing, confirming, and consecrating Bishops. But when they ceased to assemble for elections, when they entrusted them altogether to the clergy and people, when they delegated one of their own college as visitor, they paved the way for more frequent appeals to Rome, and for obtaining confirmations from thence. If the Bishops, as the canons enjoined, had held at least yearly councils, then in the case of a city deprived of a pastor, if a council had been held there, any appeal or question that arose would have been easily referred to it instead of being carried to Rome. Another result also of this infrequency or neglect of holding Councils, was the interference by the civil power in the elections and nominations of Bishops; for when they were usurped by princes, then for that reason the Bishops so nominated appealed to Rome for confirmation, and very often received consecration as well. This was notably the case in England in the reign of Henry II., and the Popes not being slow to take advantage of this increase to their power, it became by degrees a matter of necessity to appeal to the Pope for confirmation to a bishopric, and thus confirmation became separated from consecration; for as no provincial Council was assembled for the election of a Metropolitan, it was necessary to fly for refuge to a superior, who should examine and confirm the election which had been made by the Metropolitan Church. Neither was there any reason for the necessity of seeking the Pall, that confirmation of Metropolitans was assigned to the Pope; for in the first place the gift of the Pall was not a necessity to the office of Metropolitan, but a mark of honour given to him; and secondly, while the Pall was given to others who were not Metropolitans, so were there Metropolitans who did not receive it at all: amongst others were Malgerns, Archbishop of Rouen, and Stigand, Archbishop of Canterbury. In each case they were duly elected, confirmed, and consecrated; but when they applied for the Pall it was refused them. Hence on this ground also there was no need for any appeal to the Pope for confirmation. [*Cf. Thomassinus, Vetus et Nov. Discip., p.* ii., *lib.* ii., *c.* 43, *passim.*] Nowhere too was this claim of the Popes resisted more strongly than in England, nor is there "any clear instance of the Pope's confirming the elections of English Metropolitans, till the time of Richard, Archbishop of Canterbury, in 1174, and Hubert in 1191; in both which cases the elections were disputed and the difference referred to Rome.

"In the following century similar disputes afforded an opportunity to the Popes to usurp the confirmation and even the election of English Metropolitans.

"So far indeed were the Roman Pontiffs from confirming the elections of our Bishops and Metropolitans generally in those ages, that they did not even confirm in cases when Bishops were *translated,* and in which their interference would have been especially called for, had they possessed any power over our episcopal elections." [*Palmer, Episc. Vind., p.* 127.]

In proof of this we again turn to Thomassinus, who devotes several chapters to this subject, and proves that in the time of Charlemagne and his successors, "the Gallican and the German Churches always enjoyed the ancient right of making translations." And then referring to England he says, "Similarly in England also the Metropolitans, Bishops, and Kings in England possessed the same power. Oswald, a most holy Bishop of Worcester, was called to the See of York, by the election of the clergy, by the authority of Dunstan, Archbishop of Canterbury, and the command of King Edgar. 'Upon the death of the Archbishop of York, the blessed Oswald, by command of King Edgar and Saint Dunstan, Archbishop of Canterbury, and the assent of all the clergy, undertook the rule of the Church of York.' [*Surius, die* 25 *Octob., c.* 7.] Dunstan himself had formerly ruled the same church of Worcester, from which he was translated to London. 'At length the election of all turned upon Dunstan, and he was compelled by the common acclamation of all to undertake the bishopric of the aforesaid church.' [*Surius, die* 19 *Maii, c.* 26, 27, 28.] In fine, by the same unconquered power of the Divine vocation, and by the agreement of the whole Anglican Church, he was compelled to undergo the burden of the primatial Church of Canterbury. 'The unanimous election of all, calls frequently for Dunstan, etc. By this acclamation, as if by a Divine voice, he was compelled,' etc. Nor can anyone pretend that these elections were unknown at Rome, and not discovered to the Pope; since Dunstan immediately set out for Rome to seek the Pall. Wulferus and Odo, according to William of Malmesbury [*l.* 1, *Pont. Angl.*] the one Bishop of Wilton, the other of Wells, were advanced to the archiepiscopal See of Canterbury, so that the one succeeded the other. Odo refused to go, because he had never taken the monastic vow, which all the Archbishops of Canterbury had hitherto done. Yet he at length yielded to the wish of the King and the Bishops, and having set out for Fleury, and there having become a monk, returned to England and his Church: 'when the assent of all the Bishops was added to the will of the King.' To him succeeded Dunstan; to Dunstan, Ethelgar, Bishop of Chichester; to Ethelgar, Elfrid, Bishop of Wilton; to Elfrid, Siricius, Bishop of Winchester; to Siricius, Elphege, Bishop of Winchester likewise; to him Livingus, Bishop of Wells. . . . . .

"Having thus viewed Gaul, Germany, England, and having observed that, except in Gaul, Bishops and Kings did not for the most part interpose the authority of the Pope to confirm translations . . . . let us proceed to Italy," etc. [*Thomassinus, ibid., c.* lxiii., *n.* 13.] From this period (the eleventh century onwards) until the period of the rejection of Papal jurisdiction under Henry VIII., there is but little to be said; the assumptions of Papal authority, although at times resisted, increased in extent year by year; but none the less certain is it, that this jurisdiction of the See of Rome was an abuse, a violation of the canons, as uncalled for as it was illegal; and this opinion is summed up by Sir W. Palmer under the figure of an imaginary synod sitting to determine the question of the independence and inherent jurisdiction of the Metropolitans and Bishops of Great Britain, as follows: "That the decrees of the holy Fathers in the œcumenical synods, made in accordance with the law of our Lord Jesus Christ, secure the ancient and immemorial liberties and rights of all churches, whether patriarchal, metropolitan, or episcopal: that *usurpations* of authority by particular Bishops over independent churches, had ever been condemned by the Catholic Church, as contrary to the law of Christ, and fatally injurious to religion and to Christian liberty: that such usurpations ought not to prevail over the sacred canons, or to deprive oppressed churches of their rights: that the canons of œcumenical synods universally approved, and established by a custom of twelve centuries' duration, gave the election, confirmation, and ordination of the Metropolitans and Bishops of Great Britain and Ireland to their own provincial Synods: that notwithstanding these immemorial and canonical customs, the Bishop of the elder Rome had, in times of ignorance and error, succeeded in usurping the power of electing, confirming, and ordaining the Metropolitans and Bishops of Great Britain and Ireland, in violation of the sacred canons: that such a custom, however tolerated for a season by the Catholic Church, in consequence of the difficulties of the times, could never become more than an abuse, which always demanded reformation: that therefore, the Sovereigns and Bishops of England and Ireland acted laudably and piously in reforming this abuse, and in restoring the ancient, immemorial, canonical, and indefeasible rights of their churches: that the opposition of the Bishops of Rome to these measures was a renewed infringement of the sacred canons; and that the holy synod of Ephesus had long ago repealed and cancelled any pretended laws or rules which might be adduced in support of their claims." [*Palmer, Episc. Vind., pp.* 135, 136.]

Thus far I have endeavoured, by way of clearing all obstacles from the path of the due authority possessed by Parker, and consequently his successors up to the present time, to exercise real jurisdiction and mission, to trace briefly, by reference to the decrees and canons of the primitive Church, the rights and powers possessed by Metropolitans in general and those of England in particular; and I have done so for this reason, that when the usurped supremacy of the Pope was thrown off by Henry VIII., the rights and powers of the Metropolitans and Bishops of England reverted at once to what they were in primitive and Catholic times, so far at least as they were uncontrolled by any usurpation on the part of the State. How far this was the case it will be our purpose to consider later, after a review of the historical facts upon the death of the Queen Mary, and the accession of her sister Elizabeth: and I may perhaps fitly conclude this section by a passage from the well-known Tract 90, upon the xxxviiith Art.: "The Bishop of Rome hath no jurisdiction in this realm of England." After explaining what is the true meaning of the Article, the author of the tract adds: "Perhaps the following passage will throw additional light upon this point: 'The Anglican view of the Church has ever been this, that its portions need not otherwise have been united together for their essential completeness, than as being descended from one original. They are like a number of colonies sent out from a mother country. . . . . . Each Church is independent of all the rest, and is to act on the principle of what may be called episcopal independence, except, indeed, so far as the civil power unites any number of them together. . . . . Each diocese is a perfect independent Church, sufficient for itself; and the communion of Christians one with another, and the unity of them altogether, lie, not in a mutual understanding, intercourse, and combination, not in what they do in common, but in what they are and have in common, in their possession of the succession, their episcopal form, their apostolical faith, and the use of the Sacraments. . . . . Mutual intercourse is but an *accident* of the Church, not of its essence. . . . . Intercommunion is a duty, as other duties, but is not the tenure or instrument of the communion between the unseen world and this; and much more the confederacy of sees and churches, the metropolitan, patriarchal, and Papal systems, are matters of expedience or of natural duty from long custom, or of propriety from gratitude and reverence, or of necessity from voluntary oaths and engagements, or of ecclesiastical force from the canons of Councils, but not necessary in order to the conveyance of grace, or for fulfilment of the ceremonial law, as it may be called, of unity. Bishop is superior to Bishop only in rank, not in real power; and the Bishop of Rome, the head of the Catholic world, is not the centre of unity, except as having a primacy of order. Accordingly, even granting for argument's sake, that the English Church violated a duty in the 16th century, in releasing itself from the Roman supremacy, still it did not thereby commit that special sin, which cuts off from it the fountains of grace, and is called schism. It was essentially complete without Rome, and naturally independent of it; it had, in the course of years, whether by usurpation or not, come under the supremacy of Rome; and now, whether by rebellion or not, it is free from it; and as it did not enter into the Church invisible by joining Rome, so it was not cast out of it by breaking from Rome.' " [*Tract* 90, *pp.* 81, 82.]

Section V.

Had the Bishops who consecrated Parker the power to give him jurisdiction and mission as Metropolitan and primate of all England? The examination of this question is the object of the present section, and to arrive at an answer we must first consider what was the position of the Bishops of the Church of England at the accession of Elizabeth. Upon the death of Queen Mary, Nov. 17, 1558, followed a few hours after by that of Cardinal Pole, Archbishop of Canterbury, the actual position of the English Sees was as follows:—

In the province of Canterbury, five were actually vacant, by death, viz.: Salisbury, by the death of Capon, Oct. 6, 1557; Oxford, by that of King, Dec. 4, 1557; Bangor, by that of Glyn, May 21, 1558; Gloucester, by that of Brooks, Sept. 7, 1558; and Hereford, by that of Purefew or Wharton, Sept. 22, 1558.

To these were added by the close of the year, or at all events by the end of the January following, five more, viz.: Canterbury, by the death of Pole, Nov. 18, 1558; Rochester, by that of Griffin, Nov. 20, 1558; Bristol, by that of Helyman, Dec. 20, 1558; Norwich, by that of Hopton, 1558; Chichester, by that of Christopherson, 1558, or Jan. 1559. The twelve remaining Sees were London, in possession of Bonner; Winchester, of White; Exeter, of Turberville; Ely, of Thirlby; Bath and Wells, of Bourne; Worcester, of Pates; Lichfield, of Bayne; Peterborough, of Pole; Lincoln, of Watson; S. David's, of Morgan; Llandaff, of Kitchin; S. Asaph, of Goldwell.

In the province of York, York was in the possession of Heath; Durham, of Tonstal; Chester, of Scott; Carlisle, of Oglethorpe; Sodor and Man, of Stanley.

Of these seventeen, Turberville of Exeter, Morgan of S. David's, Bourne of Bath and Wells, and Heath of York, were intruders; for they were respectively appointed to their nominal Sees while Coverdale, Farrar, Barlow, and Holgate, the legitimate Bishops, were still alive, "having been pretendedly deprived by virtue of the *Regale* in Mary's reign, and certainly without any valid spiritual sentence having been passed upon them. But Bishop Farrar and Archbishop Holgate having died in the interval, the Sees of S. David's and York must be added to those which were vacant at Mary's death, while Coverdale, the Bishop of Exeter, being yet alive, and not having at this time performed any act equivalent to resignation, must be reckoned as still in lawful spiritual possession of his See." [*Union Review*, 1869.]

. Thus, out of the twenty-two Sees in the Southern Province ten were vacant, three were held by intruders, one, Llandaff, was favourable to the reaction against Rome, and only eight antagonistic, viz.—London, Winchester, Ely, Worcester, Lichfield, Peterborough, Lincoln, and S. Asaph; all of whom were in the course of the year 1559 deprived by the civil power, under the pretext of their refusing to take the oath of supremacy. As to the validity of their deprivation, it can scarcely be doubted that according to the authority of the primitive Church, their deposition was just as invalid as was the deposition of those by Mary. Spiritual jurisdiction, as it was not in the power of the State to give, so neither was it in its power to take away. This principle is defined by Dodwell, who says, speaking of the authority of anti-bishops intruded by the State, "They cannot possibly be supposed Bishops of these dioceses to which they are consecrated, till it first be supposed that their predecessors are validly deprived, and consequently that the Sees are vacant in conscience. If it should prove otherwise, the clergy and laity of these same jurisdictions will still be obliged in conscience as much as ever to adhere to their canonical Bishops till they be canonically deprived, and to disown such intruders as are put over them not only without any canonical procedure, but without any authority that can oblige in conscience. . . . . For in order to asserting such a right as this to the secular magistrate, it will be necessary to assert that the authority of the Church, even as to spirituals, is in conscience the right of the civil magistrate." [*Dodwell, Vind. of the Rights of the Church, c.* v., *quoted in a note in the Union Review, p.* 521, 1869.]

In addition to the eight thus invalidly deprived in the province of Canterbury, were the Bishops of Durham, Carlisle and Chester; but this number is reduced by the fact that before any attempt was made to fill them, or any of the legitimately vacant Sees, other vacancies occurred, by the deaths of Tunstal, of Durham, Nov. 18, 1559; Bayne, of Lichfield, about the end of the same year; Oglethorpe, of Carlisle, Dec. 31, 1559; and White, of Winchester, Jan. 12, 1560; so that there remained but six Sees in which intrusion was possible in the Southern Province, and only one, viz., Chester, in the Northern; and it is quite possible that this last Bishop (Scott) was an intruder also, for his predecessor, Coates, was intruded into Chester in 1554, the true Bishop Bird being still alive; Coates dying in 1555, Scott was appointed in 1556, in which year Bishop Bird died. Be this as it may, he soon after left the kingdom, and never returned, as did also Pates of Worcester, and Goldwell of S. Asaph.

There remain now but the Bishops of London, Ely, Peterborough, and Lincoln, to offer any opposition to Parker's election, but (as the well-known facts of his consecration prove) beyond their refusal (before their deprivation) to take any part in his consecration, they contented themselves with a silent acquiesence, and, which is of the utmost importance, outwardly accepted Parker as Metropolitan of England, inasmuch as they never raised a protest against him, or put forth any other as Archbishop of Canterbury in opposition to him.

To this state was the Church reduced by the close of the year 1559, that out of the twenty-seven Sees of the two provinces, fifteen were actually vacant, while of the remaining twelve, three, as just stated, left the kingdom of their own accord, and took no further interest in the English Church; and out of the nine, five, viz., Barlow, Scory, Coverdale, Kitchen and Stanley, supported the authority of the Crown, either actively, as in the case of the first three, or passively, as in the case of the last two, thus leaving only four in opposition, which clearly gave a majority to confirm and accept the election of the Metropolitan Parker, which the minority also tacitly accepted, for Bonner alone was suffering imprisonment, and therefore unable to offer any opposition. There is another argument, although I do not wish to lay any great stress upon it, notwithstanding that it possesses a certain force, viz., that the whole state of things was so peculiar in its accidents, Bishop after Bishop following each other in quick succession to the grave; one ecclesiastical change, before even it could take time to root itself, being superseded by another; Papal authority rejected, restored and again rejected within a few years, intrusions of Bishops being allowed in reckless defiance of Canon Law and Conciliar decrees, that it would not have been unreasonable under the circumstances, if the authority of the Crown had been invoked to supplement *mero motu* what was required. Fortunately however for us of the present day, there was no need to invoke this power; there were Bishops able and willing to fulfil all canonical requirements, for the famous *supplentes* clause, upon which so much stress has been erroneously laid by our adversaries, referred only to legal difficulties, not canonical ones; and thus when the second royal *congè d'elire* was issued, all formalities were able to be completed, and on the 17th of December, 1559, Archbishop Parker was consecrated by Barlow, Scory, Coverdale, and Hodgskin, and accepted by them, as representatives, together with Kitchin of Llandaff, of the province of Canterbury, without any voice being raised to the contrary.

If it be objected that Barlow, Coverdale, and Scory, were what are called vacant Bishops, it may be replied that the first two had been invalidly ejected from their Sees by Queen Mary, and undoubtedly were lawfully and canonically Bishops *de jure*, and as such possessed of canonical jurisdiction and mission in the province of Canterbury; and the judgment of the Catholic Church has always been, that Bishops illegally and schismatically deprived of their Sees, retained their spiritual power, as was decreed by the Council of Sardis [*Can.* 21]: "If any one hath suffered violence, and being unjustly expelled on account of his teaching and catholic confession, or for his defence of the truth fleeing dangers, being guiltless and devout, shall have come to another city, let him not be forbidden to tarry there, until he can either return, or, for the wrong done to him, obtain a remedy; for it is hard, that he who endures persecution should not be received; abundant kindness too, and good feeling ought to be shewn him."

"Moreover, if a Bishop, leaving his place, in times of persecution, ceases to be the Bishop of that place, and loses his former right and title, then the famous Athanasius [*who having been condemned by the Council of Tyre, and deposed from the See of Alexandria, was recalled from exile by the Emperor Constantine the younger, and restored to his former See of Alexandria*] ceased to be Bishop of Alexandria, and lost his right and title. For it is plain by his own confession that he fled from Alexandria, saying thus, 'I withdrew myself by stealth from the people, being mindful of the word of my Saviour, If they persecute you in one city, flee ye into another.' [*Athanas. ad. Orthodox.*] For although, the Arian faction prevailing, the Council of Tyre condemned him unheard, and deprived him of the bishopric of Alexandria; yea, though the Council of Antioch, in the presence of the Emperor Constantine, decreed, that Gregory should be appointed Bishop of Alexandria in his place; yet the Council of Sardis pronounced Athanasius Bishop of the same See, together with Marcellus of Ancyra in Galatia, and Asclepas of Gaza, his fellow ministers of Christ to be 'guiltless and pure,' 'but that those who had entered their churches, namely, Gregory in Alexandria, Basil in Ancyra, and Quintianus in Gaza, should not be so much as called Bishops, nor Christians, and that no manner of friendship should be held with them, nor any letters received from them, nor written to them.' So this most famous Council adjudged the Churches to belong to the Catholic Bishops, even at such time as they were exiled, and the Arians in possession of their Sees. For which reason, they deposed Gregory with such like, and restored Athanasius, and the rest, who had been in exile for Christ's sake, to their Churches with honour. Which very determination of the Holy Council, they signified in a Synodal epistle, to the Church of Alexandria, in these words: 'We would have you all know, that Gregory having been made Bishop unlawfully by heretics, and brought by them into your city, is deposed from the bishopric by the whole holy Synod, although in very deed he was never truly Bishop. Therefore farewell, and receive your Bishop Athanasius.' [*Athanasius, Apol.* 2.] The like is to be said of Marcellus Bishop of Ancyra, Asclepas Bishop of Gaza, Paulus Bishop of Constantinople, and others, who were persecuted for the Catholic faith, as well as Athanasius. . . . But soon after, when Eusebius, Theognis, and others, mortal enemies of Athanasius, accused him to the Emperor of threatening to hinder the carriage of corn (as usual) from Alexandria to Constantinople; and that Adamantus, Annubion, Arbathion, and Peter, Bishops, heard Athanasius himself say so, the Emperor exiled him into France, from whence nevertheless, after the death of Constantine the father, he was restored to Alexandria by the Letters of Constantine the son. Wherefore if we

are willi
admit th
possessed
being p
another,
right to th
the oth
lawfully
Episcopal
Barlow,
all other
bk. 3, c.

"Moreo
teach us
of Floren
three of th
Orders, wh
certain
indelible,
the same
any one
or that h
Layman,
that it hath
heresy,
[*Mason*,
mine,
perfect and
ments of Co
not only
he also
mine de Gla
Petrus
Altisiodoren

The posit
from the oth
Rochester, his
room of
from his
expelled

are willing to conform to the Council of Sardis, we must admit that such as in King Edward's time were lawfully possessed of bishoprics, although in Queen Mary's time being persecuted in one city, were forced to flee into another, did still remain true Bishops, and retained their right to their former titles. Wherefore, as Athanasius and the other orthodox Bishops, returning from exile, might lawfully ordain, and do all such things as belonged to their Episcopal Office, clearly in the same way it was lawful for Barlow, Coverdale, and the rest, to consecrate, and perform all other acts of their Episcopal function." [*Mason, Vind., bk.* 3, *c.* 10.]

"Moreover the holy Councils, viz. of Florence and Trent, teach us that the Episcopal character is indelible. In that of Florence, Pope Eugenius decreed as follows: 'There are three of the Sacraments, Baptism, Confirmation, and Holy Orders, which imprint in the soul a character, that is, a certain spiritual sign, distinctive from the rest, which is indelible: and therefore they are never to be repeated in the same person.' That of Trent too decreed thus: 'If any one say that Holy Orders do not imprint a character, or that he who was once a Priest may again become a Layman, let him be anathema.' . . . Whence it follows that it hath taken such firm root, that neither schism, nor heresy, nor any censure of the Church can take it away." [*Mason, Vind., bk.* 2, *c.* 11.] "Wherefore," says Bellarmine, "seeing the Episcopal character is an absolute, perfect and independent power of conferring the Sacraments of Confirmation and Order, therefore a Bishop may not only without any disputation, confirm and ordain, but he also cannot be hindered by any superior power." [*Bellarmine de Confirm., c.* 12.] And this same opinion is held by Petrus a Soto, Gregory de Valentiâ, and the schoolmen Altisiodorensis, Albertus and Adrian.

The position of Scory certainly was somewhat different from the others, for having been canonically elected to Rochester, he was translated in 1552 to Chichester, in the room of Day (who was invalidly and irregularly expelled from his See by Edward VI.); from this See he was expelled by Mary in 1554, and not suffered to return to his own See of Rochester, which at that date was not yet filled up, although immediately afterwards Griffin was nominated to it. Upon the death of Day in 1556, Christopherson was appointed, and held the See only two years. So that he (Scory) was at all events, as was also Hodgkin Suffragan of Bedford, canonically *vacant*, and as such competent to afford his aid in the necessity of the Church; for it has always been allowed that Bishops who are without actual jurisdiction over any See, in consequence of any cause which does not arise from their own misconduct, may exercise episcopal functions when permitted by other Bishops. [*Cf. Can.* 18, *Synod. Antioch. Can. Apost.*, 36.]

Upon what grounds then can Parker's consecration be pronounced irregular, and his right of mission and jurisdiction invalid? Solely upon its being proved that he himself had been guilty of schism; and, 2ndly, that all mission and jurisdiction must be derived from the Pope.

In reply to the first, as has been stated already, no separation from communion with the Church of Rome as an integral branch of the Catholic Church was ever contemplated by those who rejected the ecclesiastical supremacy of the Pope in England; neither did any such separation take place: for not only did the two communions remain united in acts of worship until the year 1570, but when that separation did take place, it was not upon any question of doctrine, but upon the refusal of Elizabeth to accept the compromise which Pius IV. offered her, that, providing she would acknowledge his supremacy, he would recognise the English Church. Clearly, had the rejection of his supremacy rendered the English Church schismatic, and this schism had been perpetuated (as it was), by many years' continuance, we can scarcely understand any common ground of union between the Church and schismatics: we should at least have expected some acknowledgment of error, some contrition for past faults, to have been exacted by the Pope first, before he could think of coming to terms. So, too, if this denial of the Pope's supremacy constituted an act of schism, then, without doubt, Gardiner, Bonner, Heath, Stokesley—in fact all the Catholic Bishops who were in England, from the time of renouncing the Pope's supremacy, to the death of Henry VIII—were schismatics likewise, and as a necessary deduction were incapable of giving jurisdiction and mission to Cardinal Pole, who succeeded Cranmer as Metropolitan; who in his turn, not having received valid jurisdiction and mission, was incapable of granting the same to his Suffragans who were consecrated by him in the reign of Mary. The truth is, that the argument of rejection of the Pope's supremacy being an act of schism, proves too much rather than too little, and is far more dangerous to its friends than to its enemies, for it throws the whole question into such a state of inextricable confusion as it would be impossible to unravel.

There is also the fact that from the period of Archbishop Parker's consecration, 1559, up to the year 1850, no attempt was made by Rome to consecrate Bishops in England, or in any way to disturb those who were in possession of the Sees. Had the Pope been satisfied that the English Church was really schismatical, some attempts, at all events, he would naturally have made to restore so great a boon as a valid episcopal succession to his followers in England; instead of this, he appointed vicars-apostolic (a titular bishop, Dr. Bishop, was sent to them in 1623, whose successor, Dr. Smith, went to France in 1629, and returned no more), and these being merely deputies of the Pope, had no episcopal jurisdiction, any more than they would have possessed it as Bishops "*in partibus infidelium*," for these had no jurisdiction at all. If it be averred that this neglect on the part of the Pope to provide Bishops in England has now been remedied, the case becomes worse for them than before; for as we deny on the part of the English Church that the rejection of the Pope's supremacy was an act of schism; and further, that the separation of the two communions, when it did take place, was their act, not ours, as S. Cyprian says of the Novatians, "We did not depart from them, but they departed from us" [*de Unit. Eccl., p.* 256]; so *they* and not *we* have been ever since in the position of schismatics in England; and therefore their present Bishops sent by the authority of the Pope since 1850 into England, are themselves intruders, and entirely incapable of exercising any jurisdiction or mission whatsoever, and indeed as a matter of fact do not possess jurisdiction *in forum externum*, but refer all matters of this kind to Rome.

On this point of intrusion into a See, Cardinal Wiseman remarks: "What will vitiate the episcopacy of a See, a province or kingdom, so as to cut it off from all participation in the rights of apostolical succession and jurisdiction? We have seen the case of the Novatians, treated in Canon viii. of Nicæa, and the decree regarding them is extremely valuable, as embodying principles acted upon most rigidly in the ancient Church. From it we are necessarily led to the conclusion, that any appointment made to a bishopric, even by valid consecration, which is at variance with the Canons actually in force in the Church, is unlawful, and leaves the Bishop so appointed void of all jurisdiction and power; so that he is a usurper if he take possession of a See. . . .

"In these and other instances, as Bolgeni remarks, there is no question of removing or deposing; but such Bishops were not supposed to have ever possessed any jurisdiction from the beginning . . . . that such nullity of episcopal nomination was the necessary consequence of the violation of the Canons in force." [*Cardinal Wiseman in Dublin Review, vol.* v., *pp.* 290, 291.]

These words, which Cardinal Wiseman intended to fall with crushing force upon the claim to jurisdiction asserted by the Metropolitans and Bishops of the English Church, will, if tested by the Canons of the Primitive Church, apply rather to those who, by command of their master the Pope, intruded themselves, after the lapse of so many years, into dioceses, to which they had not the slightest claim. Had they done so at first their action would have been intelligible, but to do so when nearly 300 years had elapsed, argues that there must have been some other motive than the mere concern for the spiritual needs of their followers here; and this motive Cardinal Wiseman supplies himself when he says in his "Appeal to the reason and good feeling of the English people on the subject of the (Roman) Catholic hierarchy," "They (the Roman Catholics) again and again were taunted with this—the Pope durst not name ordinary Bishops in England, because conscious of not having authority to do so. It was, therefore, a point of no light weight, and of no indifferent interest to (Roman)

Catholics to have this sarcasm silenced, and this obstacle removed; for many minds allowed themselves to be influenced by the apparent advantage of ecclesiastical position on the other side." [*Page* 5.]

In consequence of this the Pope, by an assumption of authority, parcelled out the land of England into fresh dioceses and nominated Bishops to each one, all of them subject to an Archbishop, whom he also styled Metropolitan; but what mission or jurisdiction could he *canonically* give them? None whatever. To see this let us apply the Cardinal's words quoted above to the test of the Ancient Canons.

The xxxvith of the Apostolic Canons says, that if any Bishop ordain in cities or villages not subject to him, "without consent of those to whom such places belong, let him, and those whom he has ordained, be deposed." The xviiith Canon of the Council of Ancyra, A.D. 314, says—

"If any being constituted Bishops, and not received by that diocese (parish) to which they were nominated, choose to proceed to other dioceses and use violence against the settled *Bishops*, and move seditions against them, let them be suspended from communion, ... but if they raise seditions against the Bishops established there, let the honour of the priesthood also be taken away from them, and let them be expelled."

The xiiith Canon of the Council of Antioch, A.D. 341, places the individual rights of Bishops beyond a doubt:

"Let no Bishop dare to go from once province into another, and ordain in the Church certain *men* to the honour of the ministry, not even if he bring others with him, unless he come invited by the letters of the Metropolitan, and of the Bishops with him, into whose country he comes. But if while nobody invites him, he goes forth in a disorderly manner for the ordination of certain persons and the regulation of ecclesiastical matters which belong not to him, the things that have been done by him indeed are null, and he also is to suffer the proper punishment for his irregularity and unreasonable attempt, being deposed forthwith by the holy Synod."

These canons at least, without reference to any others, dispose of any claim to authority which the Roman Bishops in England venture to assert; and they are adduced not in any hostile spirit, but simply in defence of what is to us of such vital importance, the apostolic succession, with all its rights and powers of our Bishops of the English Church. The second reason adduced against the validity of Archbishop Parker's jurisdiction is, that all jurisdiction flows from the Pope as successor of S. Peter. This I have stated already is an argument so untenable in the face of ecclesiastical history, that we need not further pursue it, and in fact much of what has been already said in this treatise is itself an answer to it.

To come back, therefore, to the case of Parker. The See was vacant by the death of Cardinal Pole; Parker himself was not a schismatic; and the four consecrators—Barlow, Scory, Coverdale, and Hodgkin—had full power to consecrate. Each step of that consecration was in due order; the chapter elected him, his election was duly confirmed at Bow Church, no single formality being left unobserved, witnesses being called, oaths taken, and then on the 17th of December 1559 he was consecrated at the archiepiscopal Palace at Lambeth. So far is admitted; but had the consecrators ability, circumstanced as they were, to give canonical jurisdiction? Bearing in mind that the jurisdiction which they would give was that *in forum internum*, and so was *jure divino*, there is no hesitation in saying that they, that is two of them, Barlow and Coverdale, did possess this ability, being Bishops *de jure*, although deprived of their Sees illegally at that time; and that by virtue of their apostolic commission, they were able to confer upon him universal jurisdiction and mission; and by the necessity of the case, the land being almost destitute of spiritual fathers, they were competent to confer local jurisdiction also by consecrating him to a special See, viz. Canterbury. This act of theirs was further legitimised by no exception being taken to him by those of his Suffragans in possession of Sees at that moment, who by their silence accepted him as their Metropolitan; and that being done, he as Metropolitan could fill up all existing vacancies, and give mission and jurisdiction to each Suffragan whom he consecrated.

It is sometimes said that it is an absurdity to suppose that Barlow and Coverdale could give jurisdiction to Parker, and then a few days after, the former to receive confirmation from Parker, and consequently jurisdiction and mission in a new diocese. This, however, is one of these arguments which proceed from ignorance of what jurisdiction is, and what is the effect of confirmation; but as I have already explained this particular point, pp. 12, 13, I need not further allude to it, save to remark that if Barlow possessed jurisdiction over the See of Chichester to which he was *confirmed* by Parker, and in the possession of which he died, there is an antecedent necessity as to his having possessed it before, for confirmation to a new See does not confer jurisdiction *in foro interno*, but simply assigns a fresh field wherein to exercise that power of jurisdiction which was received in consecration, the State lending the weight of her authority by nomination to a particular See to localise the exercise of jurisdiction *in foro externo.*

It was in this way that Parker also received jurisdiction *in foro externo:* the State as represented by the Sovereign had nominated him to the vacant See; by virtue of this nomination, which was the expression of the authority of the State, he was able to exercise *in foro externo* that habitual jurisdiction which he received in consecration: so that to sum up what has been said, each power of jurisdiction, viz., that given *jure divino*, and that which came from man, is incomplete without the other; for as by the first, received in consecration, he had habitual jurisdiction, which without the nomination of the Sovereign to a particular See he would have had no subjects to exercise upon; so, on the other hand, the mere nomination of the Sovereign to a particular See would have been an empty name, had he not received in consecration the power of jurisdiction, *jure divino,* as a successor of the Apostles.

It is too a curious parallelism of events which presents itself in the two cases of S. Augustine and Parker. In both the country was well nigh destitute of Bishops, in both the necessity of the case would have justified a deviation from the strict letter of the law. To S. Augustine, the Archbishop of Arles and his Suffragans, by the act of consecration, gave habitual jurisdiction and mission; Ethelbert the King, by the right of his Sovereign power, gave the field wherein that jurisdiction and mission should be exercised, viz., the *See of Canterbury*; his rights as Primate and Metropolitan were never questioned, but accepted and acquiesced in by the Suffragans of his province, whom he afterwards consecrated: so to Parker, Barlow and Coverdale gave habitual jurisdiction and mission, Elizabeth the Queen the field wherein to exercise it, viz., the See of Canterbury, as before; equally were his metropolitan and primatial rights acquiesced in, and no one questioned his power or capacity to exercise all those rights which he possessed.

Before proceeding to a consideration of the last part of the subject before us, viz., the state of the case as regards episcopal jurisdiction at the present day, and the effects which the successive Acts of Parliament passed from the time of Henry VIII. to the formation of the appellate jurisdiction of the "Judicial Committee of the Privy Council," it will be useful, as one example is worth a thousand arguments, to note briefly the arguments and salient points in the case of "Lucy *v.* Bishop of S. David's," and in doing so, I shall avail myself of the report of the case put forth by His Grace the present Archbishop of Canterbury, in his work entitled "Ecclesiastical Judgments of the Privy Council."

"This case is one of peculiar importance, not merely as almost a solitary case, since the High Commission Court was abolished, of the deprivation of a Bishop by any judicial sentence, but rather as being the only case in which the grave questions of jurisdiction, involved in such a proceeding, have been discussed in a Court of Law, and in which the arguments of counsel and the opinions pronounced by the judges have been handed down in the legal reports of the time." [*Eccl. Judgments, p.* 332.]

The points of law laid down in this case (bearing upon the question of jurisdiction) may be summed up as follows:—

"The Archbishops by the Common Law have provincial or metropolitical jurisdiction over their Suffragan Bishops.

"The Archbishop may cite a Suffragan Bishop to appear before him, or his Vicar-general.

"He may sit as judge, with or without assessors, and may hold his court in what places in his province he will.

"He may, with the assistance of assessors (or, apparently, without them), suspend or deprive a Suffragan Bishop for any offence, the penalty for which, by the ecclesiastical law, is suspension or deprivation.

"An unlimited visitatorial power implies the power of deprivation.

"An offence committed by a Bishop in some other capacity (*e.g.* as rector *in commendam* of a parish in another Bishop's diocese), is punishable in the Archbishop's Court as a breach of the duty of the Bishop's office.

"An offence punishable at Common Law is also, when committed by a Bishop, a breach of the duty of his office, and as such is punishable in the Archbishop's Court, but only with ecclesiastical censures, not as a temporal offence."

Dr. Watson, who had been appointed Bishop of S. David's by King James II. in 1687, had, according to the statement of Lucy, the promoter or prosecutor, before the commencement of the suit, been inhibited by Archbishop Tillotson, on a metropolitical visitation by that Primate, from exercising his episcopal jurisdiction, and having ordained and collated in spite of this inhibition, was suspended by the same Archbishop in 1694.

On the institution of the suit by Lucy, this suspension, at Bishop Watson's request, was withdrawn by Tenison, who had succeeded to the primacy.

The suit commenced as usual, by the Bishop being summoned to appear before the Archbishop or his Vicar-general, in the Hall of Lambeth Palace. The Bishop appeared on the appointed day, but under protest. Twenty-seven Articles were then brought in by Lucy, to which two more were afterwards added, charging the Bishop with various simoniacal acts, extortion, omission to tender oaths required by law, ordaining priest a young man under age, and converting endowments to his own use.

These allegations the Bishop specifically denied, other pleadings followed, witnesses were examined, until at length, after repeated delays—mainly, it would seem, occasioned by the Bishop of S. David's—the Bishop on the 20th of February 1699, at a Court held by the Archbishop and the Vicar-general, (which seems to have been the Archbishop's "Court of Audience") put in a protest against the Archbishop's jurisdiction, on the ground that many of *the charges* alleged were matters for the cognisance of the temporal courts; but this protest being overruled, and some of his allegations having been rejected at the same sitting, the Bishop by his proctor appealed against their rejection. The appeal lay to the King in Chancery, *i.e.* to the High Court of Delegates, and on the 13th of the following month a commission issued out of Chancery, in which five Peers, five Bishops, five Common Law Judges, and five Civilians were named as delegates to hear the appeal, with a proviso that two Commissioners at least should be present at all the ordinary acts of the Court, and not less than seven when sentence should be pronounced, of whom one must be a Peer, one a Bishop, and one a Common Law Judge."

But while the appeal was pending before the delegates, Bishop Watson (seeing, perhaps, that their decision was likely to be against him) moved in the Court of Queen's Bench for a prohibition; his counsel, Sir Bartholomew Shower, supporting the motion on several distinct grounds; upon the first of which, the denial of the lawfulness of the Archbishop's citation of him in the Hall of Lambeth Palace, that it ought to have been to the Court of Arches, the whole Court, after hearing in reply Serjeant Wright for the Archbishop, who contended, *inter alia*, that the Commissioners "had no new jurisdiction, or greater than the Archbishop," held that the citation was good, and C. J. Holt is reported to have said—"The admitting of the point of jurisdiction to be disputed, would be to admit the disputing of fundamentals, which the counsel of the other side attempt to subvert, not duly considering the respect due to the Primate and Metropolitan of England; for the Archbishop of Canterbury has, without doubt, provincial jurisdiction over all his Suffragan Bishops, which he may exercise in what place of the province it shall please him; and it is not material to be in the Arches, no more than any other place; for the Arches is only a Peculiar consisting of twelve parishes in London, exempt from the Bishop of London, where the Archbishop of Canterbury exercises his metropolitical jurisdiction, but he is not confined to exercise it there. And the citation is here to appear before the Archbishop himself or his Vicar-general, who is an officer of whom the law takes notice." [*Lord Raymond's Reports, vol.* i., *p.* 447.]

The other grounds for granting a prohibition were all

severally rejected with the exception of one, and the appeal to the delegates proceeded; and on the 8th of June 1699, the Court pronounced against the appeal, remitted the cause to the Court below, and condemned the Bishop in the costs.

The suit was then resumed in the Archbishop's court, and shortly afterwards came on for hearing before him and five Bishops, whom he called in as his assessors, viz., London, Rochester, Worcester, Salisbury, and Oxford.

The court sat very frequently, and at length the Archbishop on the 3rd August pronounced sentence of deprivation and deposition, all the Bishops agreeing with it except Rochester, who consented to a suspension, but did not think a Bishop could be deprived by an Archbishop.

The sentence is signed by the Archbishop only, the Bishops present being mentioned only as assessors.

From this sentence Dr. Watson again appealed, and on the 19th of August 1699, a second commission of appeal was issued to twenty-one delegates, all of whom except one peer and three of the Bishops had been members of the former commission of appeal.

When the delegates met, it was contended, on the part of Lucy, that no appeal lay from the sentence of deprivation. The delegates, however, held that there was an appeal, and the case proceeded.

Subsequently they decreed that Dr. Watson should be suspended *pendente lite*.

In the meantime, the Bishop had claimed to resume his Parliamentary privilege, which he had waived soon after the commencement of the suit; and the House of Lords ordered (on the 29th November, 1699), that he, and the Archbishop also, if he should see fit, should be heard by counsel at the Bar of the House. The chief ground on which it was sought to establish the Bishop's claim to resume his privilege, was the alleged illegality of the Archbishop's sentence. After hearing arguments and the opinions of the Judges, as to the methods by which, as the law then stood, a Bishop guilty of any ecclesiastical offence for which deprivation was the punishment, might be deprived, the House came to no decision on the disputed question of jurisdiction; but, after debate, the question was put, "whether the Bishop of S. David's should be allowed his privilege?" and it was resolved in the negative.

Having failed again in the House of Lords, the Bishop next moved a second time in the Court of King's Bench for a prohibition, alleging that by the Canon Law the Archbishop *alone* could not deprive a Bishop. The matter was moved several times at the bar, and the whole Court was of opinion that the prohibition should not be granted.

C. J. Holt, in delivering judgment is reported to have laid down:—

"That Archbishops and Bishops, though *pares jure divino*, are not so *jure humano*.

"That 'there are Archbishops who have authority over their Suffragan Bishops, and Primates who are superior to them.'

"That the Archbishops in England had anciently 'the same jurisdiction of supremacy as the patriarchs of Constantinople;' which having been usurped by the Pope, was long disused, but was restored by the Act of Hen. VIII. [25 *Hen. VIII, c.* 20.]

"That 'it was always admitted that the Archbishop had metropolitical jurisdiction, and the Bishops swear canonical obedience to him.'

"That 'where there is an unlimited visitatorial power, there must be of consequence a power of deprivation;' and that 'the same superiority which gives him power to pass ecclesiastical censures upon the Bishops, will give him power to deprive, it being only a different degree of punishment for a different degree of offence.' Thus the statutes '26 Hen. VIII, c. 1, and 1 Eliz., c. 1, where 'there is not one word of deprivation,' 'but only to visit,' etc., had been construed to give a power to deprive.

"That 'no other jurisdiction can be shown to which they (the Bishops) are subject; for all the same objections may be made to the power of Convocation; the notion of deprivation by which was,' the Chief Justice said, 'a new fancy of Sir Bartholomew Shower's.'

"That the peerage and temporalities of Bishops were but accessory to their office, as formerly with the mitred abbots, who were Lords of Parliament, and yet might be deprived by their visitors." [*See Lord Raymond's and Salkeld's Reports.*]

"But it was not on these grounds that the Court, though, as C. J. Holt said, 'fully satisfied that the Archbishop had jurisdiction,' based its refusal to grant a prohibition, but rather on the fact that the motion was founded on an alleged rule of the *Canon* law; viz., that the Archbishop *alone* could not deprive a Bishop. As to this, the Chief Justice stated, that 'the Archbishop by the Common Law hath metropolitical jurisdiction, and for that purpose he was constituted,' and when he did not exceed the authority which the Common Law allowed him, the breach of an ecclesiastical Canon restraining him in the exercise of that jurisdiction would be matter for appeal to the delegates, but not for a prohibition."

The prohibition being refused, the Bishop's counsel applied for a *mandamus* to require the delegates to admit the rejected allegations. This, too, was also refused; and the appeal to the delegates went on, who gave their decision on the 22nd February 1700, by which they confirmed the sentence of deprivation pronounced by the Archbishop, remitted the Cause to the Court below, and condemned the appellant, Dr. Watson, in the costs.

Such is a brief outline of this remarkable trial, the importance of which in its recognition of the Archbishop's jurisdiction it is impossible to over-estimate, and this the more because in the subsequent Acts of Parliament passed in the reigns of William IV. and our present Sovereign Victoria, for the transfer of the powers of the Court of Delegates to that of the Judicial Committee of the Privy Council, this jurisdiction of the Archbishop is in no way interfered with, but by implication, if not by express words, fully maintained.

Section VI.

So far I have endeavoured briefly to set forth the powers of jurisdiction and mission possessed by the Bishops of the Church in virtue of their apostolic commission; for as the episcopate is one, so the terms of the commission, "Go ye," etc., were spoken to each one in his single person as well as to them all in their collective capacity, for as their mission was to "all the world," so, as it was not likely (and as after events shewed was not the fact) that they would go forth to preach as a body, but each one separately, it is clear that each one regarded his commission as perfect, and as given by the Lord, the Head of the Church, to them, as being about to enter upon that work which He gave them to accomplish, separately and independently one of another. It now remains to shew by a glance at the various changes which have taken place in the Highest Court of Appeal since the rejection of the Pope's supremacy in the reign of Henry VIII. up to this day, that the jurisdiction and mission belonging to a Bishop, *qua episcopus*, that is, the jurisdiction which he acquires *jure divino*, is left untouched; while of that jurisdiction which comes to him from the Crown, no portion of its exercise is in any way curtailed, the Bishops' Courts having equally as much power now as they have ever possessed: so that were cases in the Bishop's and Archbishop's Courts unappealed against, this power would be clearly felt and acknowledged; but from the fact that the right of appeal to the Sovereign exists, and justly so, seeing it is the great privilege of the Sovereign to see that justice be done to every one; yet as this appeal to the Sovereign results in the case no longer being remitted to an ecclesiastical court, but to a secular one in which it is not a necessity that there should be any ecclesiastic at all, so the jurisdiction of the episcopate as far as regards the correction of ecclesiastical offenders is practically rendered null, a manifest contradiction to the liberty of the Church which in England, at least, has always in theory been supposed to be free, according to the first clause in the well-known Council of Brasted, held near Sevenoaks, in Kent, in the year 696, by King Withred, which declares, "Let the Church be free, and maintain her own judgments," a principle consistently adhered to, even in those early Saxon days, as may be seen in the Council of Cliff at Hoo in Kent, in 747, under Ethelbald, and at the Wittenagemote of Grately by Andover, under Athelstan, in 928, as repeated in Magna Gharta, which begins, "Let the Church be free, and hold her rights and liberties inviolate,"—and there left standing as the very groundwork of the Church's rights in all ages. So the matter remained unchanged uutil the year 1533, being in theory that ecclesiastical causes on appeal to the Sovereign should be remitted to the Archbishop's Court for final settlement, although from the usurpation of the Papal power the practice had grown up from the time of Stephen, of making the final appeal to the Pope, although any appeal to Rome without Royal assent was forbidden.

But in this year (1533) two changes were made by the Great Statute of Appeals which, as it was occasioned by the denial of justice by the Pope in the case of Henry VIIIth's divorce, "was passed to take away all appeals to Rome from Ecclesiastical Courts, which annihilated at one stroke the jurisdiction built on long usage and on the authority of the false decretals." [*Hallam, Const. Hist.*, 1, *c.* 2.] These two changes were—"1. The Upper House of the Convocation of each province was substituted for the Archbishop's Courts for certain specified classes of causes in case the 'matter or contention . . . . hath, doth, shall, or may touch the King, his heirs or successors.' 2. The power of the Crown to permit an appeal to Rome from the Archbishop's Courts was annihilated as regarded the same classes of causes in an ordinary case. So that now the Archbishop's Courts, for all the causes specified by the Act,—an appeal to Rome being forbidden,—became absolutely final by statute; unless indeed 'they touched the King,' in which case, as above said, they would be referred to the Upper House of the Convocation of that province in which they arose." [*Rev. J. W. Joyce, Civil Power in Rel. to the Church, c.* 2, *sec.* 6, *p.* 14, *London,* 1869.]

What the real legislative intentions of the times were, may be gathered from the following, the noble preamble to the Act itself, 24 Hen. VIII., c. 12:—

"Whereby divers sundry old authentic histories and chronicles, it is manifestly declared and expressed, that this realm of England is an empire, and so hath been accepted in the world, governed by one supreme head and king, having the dignity and royal state of the imperial crown of the same; unto whom a body politick, compact of all sorts and degrees of people, divided in terms, and by names of spirituality and temporality, been bounden and were to bear, next to God, a natural and humble obedience; he being also institute and furnished, by the goodness and sufferance of Almighty God, with plenary, whole, and entire power, pre-eminenee, authority, prerogative, and jurisdiction, to render and yield justice, and final determination to all manner of folk, residents, or subjects within this his realm, in all causes, matters, debates, and contentions, happening to occur, insurge, or begin within the limits thereof, without restraint or provocation to any foreign princes or potentates of the world. The body spiritual whereof having power, when any cause of the law divine happened to come in question, or of spiritual learning, then it was declared, interpreted, and shewed by that part of the said body politick, called spirituality, now being usually called the English Church, which always hath been reputed, and also found of that sort, that both for knowledge, integrity, and sufficiency of number, it hath been always thought, and is also at this hour, *sufficient and meet of itself*, without the intermeddling of any exterior person or persons, to declare and determine all such doubts, and to administer all such offices and duties, as to their rooms spiritual doth appertain, for the due administration whereof, and to keep them from corruption and sinister affection, the king's most noble progenitors, and the antecessors of the nobles of this realm have sufficiently endowed the said church both with honour and possessions. And the laws temporal, for trial of property of lands and goods, and for the conservation of the people of this realm in unity and peace, without rapine or spoil, was and yet is administered, adjudged, and executed by sundry judges and ministers of the other part of the said body politick, called the temporality; and both their authorities and jurisdictions do *conjoin* together in the due administration of justice, *the one to help the other*."

The Act then proceeds to forbid any appeal whatever to Rome, declaring that all causes determinable by any spiritual jurisdiction shall be "adjudged and determined within the king's jurisdiction and authority." And further that the appeals should be first from the Archdeacon, or his official, to the Bishop Diocesan, for the Bishop or his commissary, within fifteen days to the Archbishop of the province, without further process or appeal thereupon to be had or sued. But in case any cause, matter, or contention, shall or may touch the king, that then the final appeal should be "to the spiritual prelates and other abbots and priors of the Upper House, assembled and convocate by the king's writ in the Convocation being, or next ensuing, within the province or provinces where the same matter of contention is or shall be begun."

The following year, 1534, saw the passing of another Act, on the same subject, 25 Hen. VIII., *c.* 19, entitled "The Submission of the Clergy and Restraint of Appeals," the preamble of which, after reciting the Act of submission made by the clergy, and their promise "*in verbo sacerdotii*" to make no new Canons without the king's licence, empowers him, sect. 2, to appoint a commission of thirty-two persons, "whereof sixteen to be of the clergy, and sixteen to be of the temporality of the Upper and Nether House of the Parliament," to examine the Constitutions and Canons of this realm; and enacts that such Canons, as they "shall deem and adjudge worthy to be continued," shall be kept, and the residue declared null and void.

It next, by the 3rd section, continues the jurisdiction of the Upper Houses of the Convocation as final appeal courts, and indeed enlarges them (to use the words of Mr. Joyce) "so as to embrace all Ecclesiastical cases, 'what cause or matter soever they concerned,' if they touched the king." And then, by the 4th section, proceeds to make the important difference that, as regards all other Ecclesiastical cases, that is to say, such as did not "touch the king" an appeal should now be made to the Crown in Chancery, whence delegates were to be appointed to examine and hear the appeal. This was the origin of the famous Court of Delegates, and their decision was to be final, according to the terms of the Statute:—

"And for lack of justice at or in any the courts of the archbishops of this realm, or in any the king's dominions, it shall be lawful for the parties grieved to appeal to the king's majesty in the king's Court of Chancery; and that upon every such appeal, a commission shall be directed under the Great Seal, to such persons as shall be named by the king's highness, his heirs or successors, like as in case of appeal from the Admiral's Court, to hear and definitely determine such appeals, and the causes concerning the same. Which commissioners, so by the king's highness, his heirs or successors, to be named or appointed, shall have full power and authority to hear and definitely determine every such appeal, with the causes and all circumstances concerning the same; and that such judgment and sentence as the said commissioners shall make and decree, in and upon any such appeal, shall be good and effectual, and also definitive; and no further appeals to be had or made from the said commissioners for the same. [25 *Henry VIII.*, *c.* 19, *sec.* 4.]

It then concludes with a *Præmunire* for suing out appeals to Rome, and an enactment that appeals from places exempt, which were to the See of Rome, shall now be unto the Chancery. The commission appointed by this Act made no report during Henry's reign, but the question was not suffered to drop, for enactments upon it were repeated in 1536 and 1544, and again in the following year, 1545. [35 *Hen. VIII.*]

"Consequently upon the latter Statute, a draft of the laws was brought to such a perfection, that it wanted nothing but the royal confirmation, [*Strype's Cranmer*, 133]; and, indeed, a letter was drawn up for that purpose, for the king to sign. [*Ibid.*, *App. No.* xxxiv.] However, from some unexplained reason, this code was not published in the reign of King Henry VIII.

"Subsequently, in the Canterbury Convocation of 1547, the first year of King Edward VI., we find a petition from the Lower to the Upper House, couched in these words: 'That provision be made that the Ecclesiastical laws may be examined and promulgated according to that Statute of Parliament, in the 35th year of King Henry VIII.' [*Conc. M. B.* iv., 15.] And so the matter was again revived statutably by 3 and 4 Ed. VI., 11; and in the fifth year of that king, 1531, thirty-two persons . . . . were appointed to bring the matter to a final issue." [*Joyce*, *Civil Power*, *pp.* 59, 60.]

The result of their labours was the well-known book, entitled, "Reformatio legum Ecclesiasticarum," &c., which, although it never, owing to the early death of the young king, received royal ratification, and therefore its contents are not legally binding, yet is it of extreme historical importance as embodying the result of the labours of some of the most celebrated statesmen and divines of the day. In it, under the title, *De judiciis contra hæreses*, it declares the appeal to be, in accordance with the Statute establishing the Court of Delegates, "from the Bishop to the Archbishop, and from the Archbishop to the Crown." [*Def. leg. de Jud. cont. Hær.*, *c.* 1.] Next, when treating of the appeals more fully, under the title, *De Appellationibus*, "There the appeal from the Archbishop's Court, as settled by the Statute, 25 Hen. VIII., 19, 4, is mentioned as lying to the Crown, and then these words are put into the Sovereign's mouth: 'And when the course shall have been referred hither, we desire to conclude it by a provincial synod, if it is an important case, or by three or four Bishops to be appointed by us for the purpose,' [*Ref. Leg. De Appell. c.* xi.] . . . . thus assimilating the final resort in such causes to that which was already established for 'cases touching the king.'" [*Joyce, Civil Power*, *p.* 62.]

In the introduction to a valuable Parliamentary "Return of all Appeals in Causes of Doctrine or Discipline made to the High Court of Delegates," moved for by J. G. Hubbard, Esq., and ordered by the House of Commons to be printed, April 3, 1868, it is stated that the High Court of Delegates had, "until the year 1788, a concurrent jurisdiction with the High Court of Delegates in Ireland in appeals of all kinds from the Ecclesiastical Courts of that country. The only Ecclesiastical Court not within the appellate jurisdiction of the Delegates seems to have been the Court of High Commission, which, during the period of its existence, from 1559 to 1640, and from 1686 to 1688, derived its authority, like the High Court of Delegates, from a special Royal Commission, and would, therefore, naturally be co-ordinate with, not subordinate to, it." [*Introd.*, *p.* 3.]

"To complete the view of the judicial system which culminated in the High Court of Delegates, it should be added that each Archbishop exercised jurisdiction over the Diocesan Courts of his province, and in such peculiar courts as were exempt from episcopal, but not from Metropolitical control. In like manner each Bishop had jurisdiction in his own peculiars, and entertained appeals from the Archdeacons of his diocese." [*Ibid.*, *p.* 4.]

In the appendix to this same introduction, is an account of "the government of the Church of England," copied *verbatim* from a MS. in the Public Record Office, dated

March 24, 1636-7, and apparently draughted by Sir John Lambe, Dean of the Arches, whose name occurs very frequently in the Commissions of Delegates of the reign of Charles I., which paper is summarised in the volume of the Calendar of State Papers [*Dom. Charles I.*, 1636-7, *p.* 591, *Edited by J. Pruce, Esq.*, *V.P.S.A.*], in which the Court of Delegates is thus described :—"This Court is erected by the Statute of 25 H. 8, to hear and determine all such appeales as formerly were wont to be made to Rome. The appeale is made to (the) King in his Chauncery, thereuppon the Lord-Keeper appointeth 4, 5 or 6 of the Doctors of Lawe, and sometimes some Bishoppes and some Judges of the Common Lawe, who by the King's Commission are to heare and determine the said cause of appeale. Their proceeding is by citation *viis et modis*, etc., and their censures, as in the other Ecclesiasticall Courts, by suspension, excommunication, etc."

This Court of Delegates continued to exercise its functions until the year 1832, when its jurisdiction in causes Ecclesiastical was transferred by Statute [2 & 3 William IV., *c.* 92], to His Majesty's Privy Council.

In the previous year, 1831, a commission, which had been appointed the year before, 1830, to enquire into the proceeding and jurisdiction of the Ecclesiastical Courts, had reported that, "The Privy Council being composed of Lords Spiritual and Temporal, the Judges in Equity, the chiefs of the Common Law Courts, the Judges of the Civil Law Courts, and other persons of legal education and habits who have filled Judicial situations, seems to comprise the materials of a most perfect tribunal for deciding appeals from the Ecclesiastical Courts." A second commission, in the following year, 1832, presenting their report, recommended that Ecclesiastical appeals should be transferred from the Court of Delegates to His Majesty's Privy Council. This recommendation of theirs was forthwith carried into effect, and an Act entituled "An Act for transferring the Powers of the High Court of Delegates, both in Ecclesiastical and Maritime Causes, to His Majesty in Council," was speedily passed and ordered to come into effect on February 1 of the following year, 1833.

Had this law remained unaltered, the Church would have

had little to complain of, for the presence of the spiritualty in the Court of Appeal was plainly recognised; but, unfortunately, this Act was modified in such a manner, in the same year of its coming into force, 1833, that the constitution of the Court was entirely changed, and the appeal lay no longer to the Sovereign in Council, but to the Sovereign in and by a body called "The Judicial Committee of the Privy Council," and in this body not one spiritual person was named by the Act; which recites in the preamble:—

"Be it therefore enacted . . . . that the President for the time being of His Majesty's Privy Council, the Lord High Chancellor of Great Britain for the time being, and such of the members of His Majesty's Privy Council as shall from time to time hold any of the offices following, that is to say—the office of Lord Keeper or First Commissioner of the Great Seal of Great Britain, Lord Chief Justice or Judge of the Court of King's Bench, Master of the Rolls, Vice-Chancellor of England, Lord Chief Justice or Judge of the Court of Common Pleas, Lord Chief Baron or Baron of the Court of Exchequer, Judge of the Prerogative Court of the Lord Archbishop of Canterbury, Judge of the High Court of Admiralty, and Chief Judge of the Court in Bankruptcy, and also all persons, members of His Majesty's Privy Council, who shall have been President thereof, or held the office of Lord Chancellor of Great Britain, or shall have held any of the other offices hereinbefore mentioned, shall form a Committee of His Majesty's said Privy Council, and shall be styled 'The Judicial Committee of the Privy Council.'" [3 & 4 *Will. IV.*, *c.* 41, § 1.]

Out of these a quorum of four is selected by the Lord President of the Council, all of whom, although it is not probable, yet still it is possible, may be dissenters: and yet to the control and connection of this Court are subject the spiritual jurisdiction and superintendence of the Archbishops and Bishops of England, over the clergy and the doctrines taught by them. Certainly the Committee was somewhat improved by "The Church Discipline Act" [3 & 4 *Victoria, cap.* 86], passed in 1840, which enacted that "every Archbishop and Bishop of the United Church of England and Ireland," being a Privy Councillor, should be a member of the Judicial Committee for the purposes of that Act, viz., for the correction of clerks; but this does not give them a right to sit in general cases. But by a clause in the "Judicial Committee Act" it was enacted "that it shall be lawful for His Majesty, from time to time, as and when he shall think fit, by his sign manual, to appoint any two other persons, being Privy Councillors, to be members of the said Committee." [3 & 4 *Will. IV.*, *c.* 41, § 1.]

At the present time the Archbishops of Canterbury and York and the Bishop of London are the only spiritual persons who are Privy Councillors, and in two important cases of late years, "Gorham *v.* Bishop of Exeter," and "Liddell *v.* Westerton," not having the right to sit, they were, by virtue of the clause referred to above, present by command of the Queen, and the judgment was submitted to them before it was pronounced.

In a small treatise of this kind professing to set forth historical facts and rights, based upon Canon Law and Conciliar decrees, an individual expression of opinion as to the merits or demerits of a Court of Final Appeal, which, whether for the weal or woe of the Church, is the *law* of the land, would be out of place; and if at any time such an expression would be inopportune, it would undoubtedly be the present crisis through which the Church is passing, when from the judgment delivered in a recent case (Elphinstone *v.* Purchas) the minds of churchmen are excited, and words spoken or written possess, independently of themselves, a power and force which should only be conceded to them when they emanate from one whose authority, learning and position in the Church commend them to the consideration of churchmen. But without thus presuming to state my own opinion, I may perhaps be allowed to suggest for the anxious consideration of our rulers in Church matters as well as for those who would at any price join the enemies of the Church in their clamour for "disestablishment," whether an arrangement which should leave the Court of Final Appeal solely in the hands of ecclesiastics is in any way desirable; for it must be remembered that the English Church of the nineteenth century is not (in a political sense I mean) the Church of Apostolic times: established by law, it is endowed by law, as well as by private benefactions; and the State, as the guardian of the nation, and as bearing the civil sword, would naturally desire to control and direct all executive authority in last resort, inasmuch as appeals would be made, not only in doctrinal cases, but on questions involving law and fact. For the calmness and impartiality of the judicial mind a long course of practice, it is well known, is needed, added to which is the habit of weighing evidence which nothing but a legal education and the attendance in courts can give, and this we could scarcely expect to find in a court solely ecclesiastical; but it by no means follows that we have obtained all that the Church requires in the constitution of the present "Judicial Committee of the Privy Council," supplemented as it is occasionally by the presence of one or more of the Episcopate. And that this present Court of Final Appeal is not regarded even by its promoters in the light of perfection, is certainly more than suggested by the remarks made upon it by the late Lord Brougham, the late Bishop of London, and the late Bishop of Exeter, whose opinions I now quote, although they are already widely known.

The first, the late Lord Brougham, says—"he could not help feeling that the Judicial Committee of Privy Council had been framed without the expectation of questions like that (the Gorham case) . . . . being brought before it. It was created for the consideration of a totally different class of cases." [*Hans.*, *3rd s.*, *vol.* cxi., *p.* 629]

The late Bishop Blomfield, speaking of the creation of this new tribunal, says that the "question of doctrinal appeals was not alluded to," and adds that "the contingency of such an appeal came into no one's mind;" and in the House of Lords on the same subject, he says:—"I proceed to state some reasons why I think that the Judicial Committee is not altogether a competent tribunal for the determination of such [doctrinal] questions. (1) The judges are exclusively laymen. . . . . (2) Some of them, possibly a majority, may not only not be members of the Church of England, but may entertain opinions diametrically opposite to the Church's doctrine. . . . . (3) Putting aside the question whether the Judicial Committee can be considered as properly a Church Tribunal, I proceed to speak (4) of its *incompetency*. I am loth to use that word; but I find it difficult to employ any word which shall not be capable of an offensive meaning; and I must speak the truth. . . . . I object, then, to that tribunal on the ground that its members are not competent judges of such spiritual questions as are likely to be submitted to their decision. . . . . [Again] Every decision of a point of doctrine by the Judicial Committee would form . . . . a precedent. Such precedents settle, or modify, the law; and at last become law themselves. But it is . . . . impossible . . . . that they can give any decision upon a question which turns upon a point of doctrine without affecting to some extent the doctrine itself. . . . . In cases involving questions of doctrine, the judges who are ultimately to decide them, may by degrees alter, or modify, the laws which relate to them. But then they are not versed in divinity . . . . and the decision of purely spiritual questions should be left to spiritual judges —not merely ecclesiastical, but spiritual judges." [*Speech, pp.* 15—19.]

The late Bishop Philpott, of Exeter, (in a speech in the House of Lords, March 8, 1844, reported in the *Guardian* of April 4, 1850) says . . . . "The result of transferring the jurisdiction of the Privy Council to the Judicial Committee was, in point of fact, *to remove from the Church* the ultimate decision of all matters connected even with the very doctrines of the Church. That, he (the Bishop of Exeter) was sure could never have been intended—yet so it was; for at this hour, if a suit were brought against any of their Lordships for heresy, the Court of Appeal, which would have to decide on the matter, would be the Judicial Committee of the Privy Council. He was quite certain that this was a matter which, at the time, must have been overlooked—he was sure it was a *casus omissus*."

To these important opinions I will only add a few extracts from the well-known pamphlet by the present Premier of England, the Right Hon. W. E. Gladstone, M.P., ("Historical Remarks on the Royal Supremacy,") who says:—

"The questions that I seek to examine will be as follows:—1. Did the Statutes of the Reformation involve the abandonment of the duty of the Church to be the guardian of her faith? 2. Is the present composition of the Appellate tribunal conformable either to reason or to the Statutes of the Reformation, and the spirit of the constitution, as expressed in them? 3. Is the Royal Supremacy, according to the constitution, any bar to the adjustment of the appellate jurisdiction in such a manner as that it shall convey the sense of the Church in questions of doctrine? . . . . It was by statute that the changes in the position of the Church at that great epoch [the Reformation] were measured—by statute, that the position itself is defined; and the statute, I say, contains no trace of such a meaning as that the Crown either originally was the source and spring of Ecclesiastical jurisdiction, or was to become such in virtue of the annexation to it of the powers recited; but simply bears the meaning, that it was to be master over its administration. The powers given are corrective, not directive or motive powers—powers for the reparation of defect and the reform of abuse, but not powers on which the ordinary, legitimate, and regular administration of the offices of the Church in any way depends for its original and proper sanction. . . . . To sum up the whole, then, I contend that the Crown did not claim by statute, either to be of right, or to become by convention, the *source* of that kind of action, which was committed by the Saviour to the Apostolic Church, whether for the enactment of laws or for the administration of its discipline: but the claim was, that all the Canons of the Church, and all its judicial proceedings, inasmuch as they were to form parts respectively of the laws and of the legal administration of justice in the kingdom, should run only with the assent and sanction of the Crown. They were to carry with them a double force: a force of coercion, visible and palpable; [and] a force addressed to conscience, neither visible nor palpable, and in its nature only capable of being inwardly appreciated. . . . Lord Coke . . . . appears to proceed most unequivocally upon these principles—and to proceed upon them, not as debateable matter, but as maxims placed beyond all doubt by the theory and practice of the constitution:— . . . . that the laws Ecclesiasiastical are necessarily to be administered in Ecclesiastical Courts and by Ecclesiastical judges: as the laws temporal are 'admin*istered,* adjudged, and executed by several judges and *ministers of the* other part of the said body politic, called *the temporalty*; and both these authorities and jurisdictions do conjoin together in the due administration of justice, the one to help the other.' That 'the Archbishops, Bishops, and their officers, deans, and other ministers which have spiritual jurisdiction,' are 'the king's judges' for Ecclesiastical purposes. . . . But in the year 1833 it was enacted that all causes coming to the king in council should be tried by a committee, to be composed of at least four out of a number of persons, of whom all must be laymen: a very small proportion only could be civilians; none of the rest, except the Lord Chancellor, need be members of the Church of England. . . . Here then we have arrived at a plain and gross violation of the principle recited in the preamble of the 24th Henry VIII., that the spiritualty, according to the constitution of the realm of England, administered the law spiritual, as the temporalty administered the law temporal; the principle declared by Lord Coke, that the king administers his Ecclesiastical laws by his Ecclesiastical judges, a principle of universal application, but of the most especial and vital application, it need hardly be observed, in the trial of doctrine. And thus I arrive at the answer to my second question proposed at the outset, namely this, that the present composition of the of the appellate tribunal, with regard to causes of doctrine, is unreasonable, unconstitutional, and contrary to the spirit of the Reformation Statutes. But we come now to the third question. Is the Royal Supremacy, according to the constitution, any bar to such an adjustment of the appellate jurisdiction as should qualify it to convey the sense of the Church in matters of doctrine? I answer in the negative, and for several reasons. First, and mainly, because the Royal Supremacy was constitutionally exercised in Ecclesiastical causes by Ecclesiastical judges. . . . But secondly, are we quite sure that the appellate power is a part of the Royal Supremacy in matters Ecclesiastical at all? . . . . It is, with a view to clear comprehension of the case, a question of the highest importance. What is this appellate jurisdiction of the Crown? It did not historically flow out of the doctrine of the supremacy. It was not established in terms *affiliating* it to such a parentage. . . . At any rate *let this be observed*; the Crown possesses the appellate jurisdiction, if we construe the two Statutes 22 and 25 Henry VIII. together, under the express cover of the remarkable preamble that assigns to the spiritualty the administration of Ecclesiastical laws: and in conformity, as we have seen, with this preamble, was the appellate jurisdiction for a very long period actually exercised."

No one in reading these opinions can doubt that these illustrious persons fully recognised the right of the Church to have spiritual causes tried by spiritual persons;—how far the maintenance of that right, with a due consideration of other circumstances of the age, into which it is unnecessary to enter here, can be upheld, is the problem which now remains to be solved.

I have now endeavoured to put together the main points upon which depends the assertion that the prelates of the Anglican Church are possessed of real jurisdiction and mission, and only desire to add in conclusion the important words of one, of whom, like the aged Nestor of old, "τοῦ καὶ ἀπὸ γλώσσης μέλιτος γλυκίων ῥέεν αὐδή." [*Il.* 1, 249.]

"I have examined in turn every objection made to them [*English Orders*], and it has seemed to me that Roman Catholic controversialists took up easily any objection which might for the moment serve their turn. Cardinal Wiseman laid all aside, and took up the ground of jurisdiction. But this objection presupposes the truth of Ultramontanism. The Metropolitical See in each country has inherent jurisdiction, according to the ancient Canons. Parker was left in undisputed succession of the See of Canterbury, and his successors have the jurisdiction inherent in that See. Du Pin, when satisfied as to our orders, felt, as a Gallican, no difficulty as to jurisdiction. . . . . Bossuet says, 'This holy and Apostolic doctrine of the Episcopal jurisdiction and power proceeding immediately from, and instituted by, Christ, the Gallican Church hath most zealously retained.' 'Therefore that very late monition, that Bishops receive their jurisdiction from the Pope, and are, as it were, vicars of him, ought to be banished from Christian schools, as unheard of for twelve centuries." Def. viii. 12 in Allies, *p. 428.* [*Note to pp.* 270, 271. *The Rev. Dr. Pusey's Eirenicon.*]

BY THE SAME AUTHOR.

A DEFENCE OF HOLY ORDERS IN THE CHURCH OF ENGLAND; together with the Statutes, Documents, and Incidental Evidence; to which is prefixed (by permission of his Grace the Archbishop of Canterbury) a Photozincographic Fac-simile of the Record of Archbishop Parker's Consecration from the Lambeth Registers. Latin and English, 150 pp., folio. Price 30s.

J. & J. H. PARKER, 377, Strand, London.

Also,

FOUR LETTERS OF PERE GRATRY TO THE ARCHBISHOP OF MALINES ON PAPAL INFALLIBILITY. Translated from the French. Price 3s. 6d.

Also,

LETTERS OF THE ARCHBISHOP OF MALINES TO THE BISHOP OF ORLEANS AND PERE GRATRY. Translated from the French. Price 1s. 3d.

HAYES, Lyall Place, Eaton Square, London.

G. WAKELING, Brighton.

CPSIA information can be obtained
at www.ICGtesting.com
Printed in the USA
BVHW042327150223
658636BV00021B/369